STANLEY DAYO

Manley Hot Springs

STANLEY DAYO

Manley Hot Springs

SPIRIT MOUNTAIN PRESS
P.O. BOX 1214 FAIRBANKS, ALASKA 99707

ISBN: 0-910871-11-6

Interviewing and Editing:
Yvonne Yarber and Curt Madison

Photography:
Curt Madison (unless otherwise noted)

Material collected in Manley Hot Springs April 1979, November 1981, January 1984.

Manuscript approved by Stanley Dayo January 1984.

**Library of Congress
Cataloging in Publication Data**

Madison, Curt
Yarber, Yvonne
    Dayo, Stanley - Manley Hot Springs. A
    Biography
    YKSD Biography Series
    ISBN 0-910871-11-6

1. Dayo, Stanley 2. Mining, Trapping
3. Alaska Biography

SPIRIT MOUNTAIN PRESS
P.O. BOX 1214 FAIRBANKS, ALASKA 99707

Produced and Funded by:
Yukon-Koyukuk School District of Alaska

Regional School Board:
Luke Titus - Chairman
Donald V. Honea - Vice Chairman
Neil Morris - Secretary
Patrick McCarty - Treasurer
Eddie Bergman
Cheryl DeHart
Patrick Madros

Superintendent: Joe Cooper
Assistant Superintendent: Fred Lau
Project Coordinator: Don Kratzer

Supplemental funding:
Johnson O'Malley Grant - EOOC14202516

Cover Photo:
Stanley Dayo on his cabin porch November 1981. Photo by Curt Madison.

Frontispiece:
Stanley Dayo with his daughter Dixie in front of his cabin at Manley Hot Springs April 1984. Photo by Curt Madison.

Acknowledgements

This book would not have been possible without the help of many people during the four years of its preparation. Bea Hagen typed the transcripts of hours of interviews with Stanley. Liza Vernet donated her time proofreading and giving valuable advice. Bob Maguire, the itinerant administrator (who knows where he is now), invented this project. Renee Blahuta, University of Alaska Archivist searched her archives. Norm Suckling and Martha Boyle allowed use of their fine old photos. Joe Cooper, Fred Lau, and Mavis Brown provided administrative acumen. And the Regional Board of the Yukon-Koyukuk School Board continue to support local curriculum. Finally the people of Spirit Mountain Press Larry Laraby, Doug Miller, and Eva Bee moved the manuscript to finished product.

All royalties from the sale of this book go to the Yukon-Koyukuk School District for the production of more autobiographies.

This is the first printing of this book. Please let us know about any corrections for future printings.

Foreword

This book is the eighteenth produced by the Yukon-Koyukuk School District in a series meant to provide cultural understanding of our own area and relevant role models for students. Too often Interior Alaska is ignored in books or mentioned only in conjunction with its mineral resources such as the gold rush or oil pipeline. We are gauged by what we are worth to Outside people. People living in the Interior certainly have been affected by those things but also by missionaries, wage labor, fur prices, celebrations, spring hunts, schools, technology, potlatches, and much more. For residents, Interior Alaska is all of those things people do together, whether in the woods, on the river, in the village or on Two Street. It's a rich and varied culture often glossed over in favor of things more easily written and understood.

This project was begun in 1977 by Bob Maguire. Representatives of Indian Education Parent Committees from each of Yukon-Koyukuk School District's eleven villages met in Fairbanks February of 1978 to choose two people from each village to write about. A variety of selection means were used—from school committees to village council elections. Despite the fact that most of the representatives were women, few women were chosen for the books. As the years passed, more women were added to give a more complete accounting of recent cultural changes.

It is our goal to provide a vehicle for people who live around us so they can describe the events of their lives in their own words. To be singled out as an individual as we have done in this series has not always been comfortable for the biographees, particularly for those who carry the strong Koyukon value of being humble. Talking about oneself has been a conflict overridden by the desire and overwhelming need to give young people some understanding of their own history in a form they have become accustomed to. A growing number of elders who can't read or write themselves think young people won't believe anything unless it's written in a book. This project attempts to give oral knowledge equal time in the schools.

As materials of this kind become more common, methods of gathering and presenting oral history get better. The most important ingredient is trust. After many hours of interview, people often relax to the point of saying some personal things they prefer left unpublished. After editing the tape transcripts we bring the rough draft manuscript back to the biographees to let them add or delete things before it becomes public. Too often those of us living in rural Alaska have been researched *on* or written *about* for an audience far away. This series is meant to bring information full round--from us back to us for our own uses.

Too many people in the Interior have felt ripped-off by journalists and bureaucrats. Hundreds pass through every year, all wanting information and many never to return. Occasionally their finished work may find its way back to the source only to flare emotions when people feel misrepresented. Perhaps a tight deadline or the lack of travel money may be the excuse for not returning for verification or approval. That is no consolation for people who opened up and shared something of themselves and are left feeling betrayed. We work closely with the biographees to check facts and intentions. The books need to be intimate and daring but the last thing we want to do is make someone's life more difficult. We need to share information in a wholesome way. After all, we're all in this together.

Comments about the biographies, their use, corrections, questions, or anything else is welcome.

Curt Madison
Yvonne Yarber
December 10, 1982
Manley Hot Springs
Alaska 99756

Table Of Contents

Introduction

Stanley Dayo came to Alaska in the 1930's as a young man. He's spent his adult life in the woods and goldmines of the Interior. Living in Manley Hot Springs longer than anyone else, he's gained the respect and friendship of the town's people who refer to him as "the mayor".

Stanley tells of his early days as a "bohunk" walking the country, trapping, living off the land and meeting folks who have become historical characters to younger people and newcomers. He has seen the countryside, lifestyles and laws change dramatically in the past fifty years. Still his manner is easy going and kind.

This book is written in Stanley's language style which is rich with expressions that come from logging camps, goldmines and his Slavic heritage. His story is one more dimension of Alaska's Interior history.

Glossary

birds — slang for man

CCC — Civilian Conservation Corps, instituted during the Great Depression for unemployed workers

cleanup — taking gold out of the riffles of a sluice box

gandy dancing — gandy dancers worked as section hands laying tracks for a railroad

giant — high pressure water hose for washing dirt or gravel in a placer mine

guyline — a rope or cable used to stabilize a pole

hard rock mine — a mining operation that digs through bedrock following mineral veins

Hoot — nickname for the Hutlinana River

hunky — person of Eastern European descent, bohunk, slav

isinglass — a tough transparent material made from air bladders of certain fish or mica. Until plastic was invented, isinglass was in common use as storm windows and side curtain windows on early automobiles. The small windows in stove doors were made of mica.

lay — an agreement to work someone's mining claim for a percentage of the take

placer mine — a mining operation extracting minerals, usually gold, from the gravel layer just above bedrock, occasionally gold is mixed in the gravel all the way down to bedrock.

PX — Post Exchange where goods can be purchased by people in the military and their dependents

rocker — a hand operated screen requiring water to separate gold bearing sand from gravel

sniper — a person using a rocker to go through someone elses tailing for gold left behind, a small operator

tiehackers — workers using broad axes to cut and lay railroad ties

WPA — Work Projects Administration, a federal agency during the Great Depression that organized jobs to create employment

Local Area

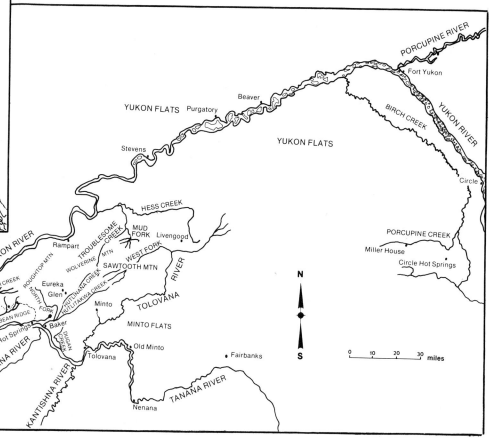

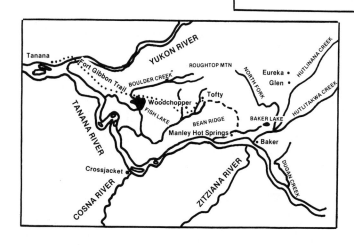

10

Chapter One: Wisconsin to Washington

A Kid In Wisconsin

I was born 1913. Steven's Point, Wisconsin. It was a sawmill town with lots of logging around. Three big paper mills and quite a few sawmills. A few factories around. Farming outside of town. At that time the town was about 12,000 population. Milwaukee was the closest big city about 150 miles to the south.

My mother was a housewife all the time. She just, well, the old timers them days, stayed home and done their housework. Another thing, my mother never got out of the state of Wisconsin till she was over 70. Then my niece took her to Minnesota. They never traveled around much, most of them people.

Dad got around more before he was married. He used to work in the woods in Michigan and in the mines in Minnesota. It was easier for a man than a woman. A woman didn't move around like a man you know. My mother was raised out in the boondocks you might say. On a ranch way out and didn't hardly have any education. No schools, you know. They had to get out and work. Hard to make a living on a lot of those farms.

After Dad got married he worked in a lumberyard. He was the boss, but still he wasn't making much money. He had three or four guys working there and he worked right alongside of them for three and a half bucks a day. And that's ten hour days, too. Six days a week. No unions around and no big money anyway. Sawmillwrights and head sawyers made the most money. My uncle was one. He got a dollar an hour and they throught that was real big money for them days.

We'd go in on the old logging works and cut out the second growth for cordwood. We'd haul wood to the mills, too, on shares. They make lumber and we get half of it back.

Dollar and a quarter a cord for stove wood was the going rate and no chain saw. That's with a bucking saw. Loggers in the woods were getting a dollar a day, thirty dollars a month plus their room and board.

I was in those logging camps, myself. I seen them. We'd go out to my Uncle's land and haul saw logs to a mill with horses for seven or eight dollars a thousand board feet. A thousand board feet is about the same as a cord of wood. That's all we got.

At fourteen or fifteen I grew up to be just as big as I am today. By seventeen I could get a job with men. They weren't strict them days about age. When you went to work, if you looked big that's all that mattered. They just wanted some help.

The unions first started coming in when I was a kid. The old IWW's, Industrial Workers of the World. They was the ones started getting going for better conditions and higher wages. There were fights about it. The loggers bucking the mill owners and strikes and stuff. After the strikes they started getting better conditions in the camps. Some of them were pretty poor. Logging camps had big bunk houses for two or three hundred men and no showers. That's what they were bucking for — better conditions. And all the camps were lousy. Lice in your bed and lice in your hair.

Since we lived in town we didn't have farm chores to do but we had to get water and wood. We had wells out in the yard and a hand pump for water. What chores we had to do we did. When our parents told us something we had to do it and that wasn't thinking about it or do it later. You went and done it. Or else.

All of us kids were always wishing for snow so we could make some spending money. We'd go uptown where all the business people had to keep their sidewalks cleaned off. If we made fifty or seventy-five cents that was real good. And we had to shovel a lot of snow for it, too. But then a dollar was a lot of money for a kid about ten or twelve them days.

We'd pay a dime for a movie and a nickel for a bag of popcorn. Hot dogs for a nickel and big candy bars. O Henry and Babe Ruth were popular bars. There was Hershey, too, but O Henry and Babe Ruth were the best. Of course, there was peanuts around.

A bunch of us kids would get to help some of the men build ski slides. We'd get poles and scrap lumber and make a scaffold on a hill. High and steep for skiing and jumping. We were all pretty good at it and then there were a lot of experts, too.

My dad owned his own home. We lived right on the Wisconsin River. It seems it was about as wide as the Tanana River. Summertime there was a lots of fishing and swimming in the lakes and creeks and the river. We all had boats. But no power them days. It was all oars and paddles. No kid had an engine. If you went any place you walked or you took the boat. That's a fact. Some people had Old Town canoes made over in Maine, but a lot of people made their own skiffs. My old man made a couple boats for us kids when we were growing up.

The ones he made were scow nose, anywhere from twelve to sixteen feet long. Most of the boats were made of lumber. Very few metal boats around. Some few people had outboards. But them old Evinrudes, you know, you was cranking on them most of the time. And they were small, not much horsepower. They were just a little bit better, when you got 'em running, than a pair of oars. That's about all. Most people if they had an engine it was an inboard. Those were pretty reliable.

Us kids would take off with just our fish poles and something to eat and go up the river all day. Come home with a whole sack full of fish. It was real good fishing for pike and blue gills, crappie and muskies, perch and bullheads, and all that stuff. We'd take off walking across from one creek to another and over to a lake. We knew where all of 'em were, you know, and we'd fish them. Go anyplace. People'd never bother you. There was farmers around, but nobody'd bother you then. It wasn't like nowadays. They didn't bother a kid much.

Same way we'd hunt. When we got older and had .22's, we'd go after rabbits. We'd go a lot with older boys or men. Sometimes about two or three of us would go with someone's father or uncle. We'd do that a lot like on Sundays and Saturdays when we had our days off school. It was pretty good hunting for birds, ducks and grouse. Partridges, prairie chickens and a lot of rabbits and squirrels. Grey squirrels and fox squirrels. Of course, there was quite a few deer out in the old logging works above from where we lived. Then in the winter it was skating and skiing. That was our big fun.

Us kids would run around and do a little trapping — muskrats, mink, and stuff like that. In the late 20's fur was pretty good. You'd get couple dollars for a rat. It was a lot like getting rats in Alaska, but we never shot them, just traps. We started in the fall and went all winter.

School

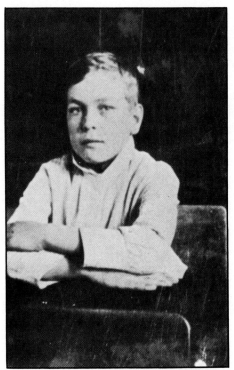

I went to school up to seventh grade. That last school I went to was Grant School. One teacher had about fifty of us in the sixth and seventh grades together. Must have been a lot of kids because there were six or seven schools in that one town including a high school and a Catholic School.

The best thing I remember about it was the ball teams. We played basketball and after I left school we all had our own baseball teams.

A lot of kids went on to high school, but a lot of kids didn't either. To be honest I didn't like school. I was kind of rambunctious. I wanted to do something on my own. Get out, work, and make a few dollars. Those days a lot of us didn't want to go to school. I wasn't the only one. For me I didn't have to go out and work, because my dad was making plenty of money and most of my brothers and sisters were grown up. I was the youngest. But a lot of my friends had younger kids in the family and they had to get out and

Stanley Dayo in school, 1920's.

help make money to support them. It was hard going there.

My parents rebelled. They wanted me to go on in school, but I wasn't interested. Just me and one sister left home. All my brothers had pulled out already. They scattered all over the county. One was in Washington, some stayed in Wisconsin but moved north in the state. Another one to Minnesota. They just went wherever the work was.

Going West For Work

I left Wisconsin heading west to see my brother. The first place I stopped was a sheep ranch in Montana. The rancher had a lot of sheep out in the hills and we put up hay for him for the winter. After that I went down to the coast to Mt. Vernon, Washington.

There was lots of farming there. Lots of work. You could always pick up a job working for those farmers picking spuds or something. And there was a big cannery in the town. All these farmers contracted with the cannery to raise beans and strawberries and that. In the fall they had to hire a lot of pickers. A good worker could make up to three and half bucks a day for eight hour days. I remember one place we went picking beans I was making about two and a half a day. There were a lot of older people working there but, of course they didn't make that much. Some of the women were real fast pickers. They'd make three or three and a half a day. That was real good money then.

At the same time you got to remember

Stanley Dayo.

"That's in Washington where I lived with my oldest brother John. That's his wife, John and some neighbors holding some martens he caught up in the hills. Right back behind the house you can see a little bit of the cabin I lived in and all those tree stumps. That's why they called places like that 'stump ranches' ''.

prices were a lot lower, too. You could get Levi's for a dollar and a half, overalls were eighty-five cents. A good clean room and a bed was thirty-five cents a night. You could get four hot cakes, two eggs, and coffee for a dime in Spokane. All you could eat of stew for fifteen cents. At those prices cooks weren't getting much for their long hours. Maybe a couple bucks a day is all.

I had a cabin belonged to me on my brother's place. We stayed there all the time, me and another brother. The cabin was made out of shakes, big cedar split shakes. It don't get cold in that country. You don't need a warm cabin. No insulation or anything. We had lumber for floors. It was fixed up good inside. Then all we needed was a heater. We cooked on wood, of course. It didn't take much of a stove either. We could heat it with the cook stove alone. There was hardly any snow. I remember some years it didn't snow at all in the valleys. Up in the hills there'd be snow all the time, but it was rain in the valleys.

It was easy country to live in. You could raise anything easy. Good land. Spuds, carrots, rutabagas, cabbages, and beans all growed good. Mostly we planted between the stumps of the logged off land. Stump ranches we called them. People raised chickens, cows, and a few pigs. They's just knock 'em on the head anytime they wanted a little meat. And a lot of fish. We lived right off the Skagit River and a lot of salmon used to come up there and spawn. We'd get them anytime we wanted. And we went after steelhead on the riffles. Just put a big hook on our pole and gaff 'em.

It was early 30's I got to Washington. Depression time. Things were tough around the country. Work was real hard to find. If you did find a job there wasn't much money in it. And if you had a job you had to produce or there was a bunch standing around to take your place. All through Hoover's years things were tough. Then when Roosevelt took over he started getting the ball rolling. He got the WPA and CCC camps to put people to work. He took all the young fellas out of town and put them to work cutting trails and fire lines and stuff in the woods. They were getting their room and board and maybe a dollar a day. I never worked in one myself, but that was the beginning of things getting better.

I was probably one of the lucky ones with a lot of jobs. When I lived up the Skagit River there was always something coming up, some kind of work once I got acquainted around. I'd go to work for the Forest Service packing supplies out to their camps. We'd get thirty-five cents an hour fighting fire and I got one job cutting a right-of-way for a road into Mt. Baker National Forest. That was a state job and they couldn't pay any less than four dollars a day. That was considered real good pay. Eight hours a day, seven days a week. I worked at it for six months and made all kinds of money.

For two guys in the early 30's we could live fine on ten dollars a month plus our garden. Eggs were eight cents a dozen. Bacon was eight cents a pound. Flour and beans were a cent a pound if you bought 'em. Rice was cheap and sugar and macaroni. Milk and butter from the farmers wasn't bad. Canned fruit like pineapple was ten cents a can, but every stump rancher had an orchard. In fact a lot of them were abandoned by guys that got disgusted with the country and left. They were just growing to be picked.

All the jobs I ever had were in the woods cutting and falling logs. Then I was trapping a little out there, too. Me and Hubert Berry, another kid eighteen years old, went up in the Cascades after marten a couple winters. There were a lot of marten but it was tough trapping up and down in those hills. We trapped the same way you do here with number one and ought traps, but all pole sets. It was nothing to get fifteen or twenty feet of snow. We set under big cedars and fir trees, but we still have to raise the poles up. You could get four or five feet of snow some nights.

Walking was the only way to go there. No dogs. All snowshoes up and down hills. We took our supplies out in the fall with pack horses then came back later when the fur was prime to start trapping.

The Forest Service used horses to supply their fire-watch towers. All summer they kept them in a high meadow feeding on wild pea vine vetch. Deer ran around right amongst them. The Ranger said we could use the horses to get our stuff out if we brought them down to Marblemount afterwards.

We started packing from the end of the road at Diablo Dam. Late October and it had been snowing in the pass. Hubert was leading on his big iron gray, breaking out the trail in four feet of snow. That damn horse would just plunge on ahead. I'm amazed we made it. Then down in the valley out of the pass, we followed Big Beaver Creek to the Skagit River on bare ground. No snow at all.

We could only stay six weeks in that high rough country before we had to get out. As soon as it started to thaw snowslides were everywhere. We got sixty-eight marten and didn't seem like we worked at it very hard. Caught a wild cat, too. Between the two of us we had two or three hundred traps and fifty or sixty miles of line. I guess we had that much, but it wasn't in a straight line. We'd have camp on one creek, go up and back that creek, then go on ten miles and have another camp.

We built some of the cabins and rented the others from the Forest Service. They cost five dollars a year and came complete with stoves and cooking utensils. We trapped right up to the Canadian border. There were a lot of Canadian trappers on the other side but on our side the closet guy was Herman Rohde about fifteen miles away on Big Beaver Creek. My partner and I got along in the woods pretty good. We had plenty of food and there were always deer around.

There were game laws and hunting seasons, but nobody paid much attention to them. There was one game warden in Mt. Vernon and that's all. He used to come around now and then, but those guys were tough on him. Game wardens had to watch themselves. They didn't go around making too many pinches. People didn't like them. Didn't want them around.

After we trapped about six weeks we came back down to the valley and looked for other work. It was prohibition them days and no bars to go in to celebrate selling furs. There'd be a few dances and pool halls to go to and stuff like that but we wouldn't hang around long. After a few days we'd go right back out to the ranches and stay there.

I finally left that place in '33. Forty years later I went back. Boy, there was a real change. More people around and all the timber logged off. In my day we were logging in the valleys, now they're up the hillsides and all over. All the virgin timber, the big stuff, was gone and they were logging alder and maple and second growth cedar and fir. You see roads all over and trucks.

I figured it'd change but not as much as it did. Logging's different now, than when we were there. We just took the big stuff. Six or eight foot through was nothing. Now they take everything down to four or five inches. They got different sawmills now. Stud mills that cut nothing but two-by-fours and two-by-sixes and chip all the rest. They knock the bark off and send the chips to the paper mills. They take stuff we never even looked at.

And it was all steam high leads. Cats just started coming in. Now its all cats and rubber-tired skidders. Build a road to the logs and load them right on trucks. We used to rig a spar tree, guy it off, and run our block up to the top. A cable went from the engine on the ground up to the block and half a mile into the woods. That cable hooked to a choker and the log snaked all the way back to the landing. It's still hard work, though, no matter how you do it.

We didn't even have chain saws. All two man crosscut saws, misery-whips standing on springboards. It was hard work but that was the only work around. It's all people done in Washington, Idaho, and Oregon. If you wasn't a timber beast, a logger, you was nothing.

Photo by D. Kinsey. Whatcom Museum of History and Art.

Washington loggers circa 1910. "I cut a lot of those big trees down in my time. That's the kind of saw we used, "misery whips". We'd stand on those springboards like the guy on the left, make the bottom cut with a two-man-saw and then under-cut. It's easy logging now compared to long ago."

Chapter Two: Coming To Alaska

Leaving On The Boat

When I left Washington to come up here, I quit that country. I had met different guys in Washington, fishermen and stuff, that had been up here on the coast. My neighbor in Marblemount was a doctor in one of the canneries. He worked just in the summers and then moved out by me in the winter to get away from it all, I guess. Doc Hawkins was his name. Jobs weren't easy to come by in the canneries, but he had quite a bit of pull. We got acquainted doing things together fishing and stuff. He said if I ever wanted a job he could get me one. But me and my brother Frank didn't want to be obligated to anyone so we made a few dollars, held on to it, and came up on our own.

Lot of guys wanted to come north because of the big wages, but I was always interested in the trapping. I met a guy, Frank Bebee, trapping in the Cascades who was up here for a few years. He told me about it and got me interested. I wanted to see the country. Just more or less interested in trapping and prospecting. I beat around prospecting a little in Washington, but never found nothing.

I come up by steamboat on the *S.S. Alaska*. Seven days from Seattle to Seward. That included stops

Stanley Dayo.

"That's my brother Frank goofing around in Washington, 1931.

21

along the way to load and unload stuff. The only rough weather was in the gulf. The boat was full of fishermen and clamdiggers going to Cordova and they all got seasick. Me and my brother and a couple others were the only ones didn't get sick. Didn't seem to bother him or me.

You could come up steerage, or first class if you wanted to spend the money. We came steerage. It wasn't bad. Quite a few guys down there all right and just bunks. Wouldn't say the food was the best but you could make it. Altogether the fare was just under forty-five dollars. Only thing we needed was our own bedding. Weather was nice when we left Seattle but there was quite a bit of snow when we landed at Seward. April of '33.

All the big stampedes were over by the time I hit the country, but the camps were still going pretty good. Fairbanks was a big camp with the dredges in there. Eight or ten of them working. This camp, Manley, was a good one and Livengood, Circle, all over. They were still doing a lot of mining. No big wages though. Five dollars a day. Or six for long ten hour days. Some places they was working you twelve. And you had to work, too. Hard work. No bulldozers them days. Couple years later they started bringing them in.

Looking for Work

From Seward we went to Anchorage by train. Lot of snow there and a lot of guys looking for work. It wasn't a very big town, I can tell you that. After you left 5th Avenue it was all brush, just a few scattered shacks. We rented the upstairs floor of a cabin on 9th Avenue. All we needed was our own bedding for ten dollars a month. It was a good deal. Right now you couldn't sleep under a bridge for ten dollars a night.

There was only two hangouts around there, the Panhandle and the Alaska Club on 4th Avenue. All the fishermen, trappers and tiehackers hung around there. Fishermen were waiting for the fishing to open up. Guys waiting to go to work on the railroad, and then there was a couple hard rock mines, the Lucky Shot and the Independence. The railroad had an office they hired out of.

We only had about a hundred fifty dollars between Frank and me. We were trying to get on somewhere, but nothing going on. The only thing you could do was come to town and wait for some boss to come around looking for men. Or if there was a job, somebody you knew would wise you up to it. But we never got out on anything.

There was an Italian guy named Julio staying in the cabin on 9th Avenue with us. Waiting for work we'd gamble in the bars playing gin rummy for ten cents a hand. First I'd play until my luck ran out, then Frank. Finally Julio would get in and he almost always won. He loved to gamble. Pretty sharp, too. One of us always came out good, we were living on our winnings from that game.

Julio liked to drink, too. The guy we were renting the cabin from was a bootlegger. When Julio won a few hands of rummy he'd go get a pint and we'd all have a drink. Nothing but bootleg dives all around there. It was a wide open town.

It didn't bother me because I was used to it around in the Western states. Bumming around with a bunch of rough characters. I had a lot of experience by the time I was twenty. I was onto the ropes.

There was always a lot of people coming up looking for high wages and easy gold. A lot of them were real gullible. They thought every creek in the country was full of gold. All you needed was a pick and a shovel. There was a lot of them believed that, you know. I met a lot of them. Well, you meet 'em right now even. They think that under every bush is a pot of gold, just about. Behind every rock.

We couldn't get on in Anchorage so we went to Fairbanks. The FE Company was only hiring guys that worked for them years before. No chance of getting into a mine there so we took off walking to Circle.

We had our bedroll, of course, some clothes and a little grub. Mostly hot-cake flour, bacon and rice, coffee, tea, salt and a little sugar. Something easy to pack. That was about the standard fare. I don't think we had over 50 pounds apiece with all our bedding and the ammunition. I probably had more ammunition than anything else. We used Trapper Nelson pack boards and strapped our bedroll on top. Spring of the year. A nice trip.

They didn't open the roads them days. They just let them melt out in the spring. Frank and I met a couple other guys on the road so we all took up together. At that time the Road Commission had cabins every ten or twelve miles for their summer crews. Mail carriers hauling mail from Circle to Chatanika with dogs used them, too. We'd make one of those camps and stay around a while. We had some grub with us and we'd shoot a little game on the road, ptarmigan and stuff like that. Right at the foot of Eagle Summit we ran into lots of caribou. We had caribou meat from there on. I didn't worry about nothing them days. I knew we'd live somehow. We wasn't exactly broke yet, but getting pretty close.

We thought we could get on at a mine around Circle, but again there was nobody hiring. Circle was the headquarters for guys at Miller House, Mastodon Creek, Deadwood Creek, and Porcupine Creek. Rassmusson was freighting there and guy by the name of Alexander was the N.C. agent. The rest of the town was full of trappers. All those towns along the river were full of trappers.

That winter the deputy marshall McClain had died and his wife was pulling out. We did some work for her and she paid us off with an old poling boat. We patched it up and decided to float downriver. The flats were full of ducks and geese. You couldn't go hungry there.

The first stop was in Fort Yukon. Three stores and lots of people. Natives and Whites. All trappers. I met Jimmy Carroll. He had been a trapper before he started his store. Later I got to know his son when we were in the army together at Ladd Field.

Next was Beaver. A Jap named Frank Yasuda had the store there. He had a cabin behind the store where all the transients stayed. He let us stay long as we wanted. ''Rest up,'' he said. So we hung around three or four days.

Below Beaver was Purgatory, a roadhouse run by the Yanert brothers. They had a lot of carvings and curios there. Right on the bank he had a big devil standing. The steamer *Yukon* had a regular schedule from Dawson to Nenana with tourists and freight. As the boat got closer one of the Yanerts would be back in the brush with a wire to the devil. He'd pull his wire and the devil would wave the boat in. I think that devil is in the museum in Fairbanks now.

We finally got to Rampart and stopped floating. The four of us were still together and we got a lay off this old colored guy Gene Swanson who had some claims there. We worked underground all summer and by the time we got through between me and my brother all we had 80 dollars. Not much gold.

Frank and I went up Troublesome Creek in the fall, built a cabin, trapped and prospected. One guy went back to Fairbanks and out to Minnesota. The other guy, Leo Elg, we called him American Creek Shorty later on, built a cabin about three miles from us and prospected that winter, too. There were more Natives than White guys in Rampart, but a small camp like that everyone got along real well. Mostly the guys were trappers, Evans, Mayos, and Woods families. They trapped in the winter. Fished, worked in the mines, or cut cordwood in the summer.

"That's in front of Frank Yasuda's cabin the year we floated down to Beaver. Frank Yasuda was a real good old guy and let us use the cabin. Leo Elg "American Creek Shorty", Tom Donahue, and me."

No Picnic

When we come over from Rampart to Livengood it was the winter of 1934. Livengood was a pretty big camp then. It had a couple of stores and a post

L-R: Frank Dayo, Tom Donahue, and Stanley Dayo on Hunter Creek, six or seven miles from Rampart. "That's the first summer when we mined and didn't do very good, 1933. The cabin belonged to an old German who moved to Fairbanks and started a bakery and restaurant. You could get a big sandwich and cup of coffee for twenty-five cents."

"Fall, 1933 on our way to Troublesome Creek to prospect. We're stopped on the trail at Jack McGinty's cabin, he was trapping there."

office. Must have been three or four hundred people mostly working in the mines, drift mines. Jay Livengood, the guy they named the town after was still there mining. And Teddy Hudson, Jay and Teddy were the discoverers of the camp. Teddy's brothers, Jim and Cliff were mining. Cliff's son, Albert, was in the freighting business hauling with a team of horses from Dunbar.

Livengood and Spaul were drift mining, so were Tony Silver, Tony Zuber, and Tony Benny. Then there was Anderson and Peterson all working year round underground drifting. In the summer, guys ran open cuts hydraulicing on Ruth, Amy, Lillian, and Wilber Creeks. All of them, drift or hydraulic, were placer mines.

You know what drifting is. First, you have to dig a shaft to bedrock where your pay is. Then pick a tunnel, drift, along the bedrock following the paystreak. To get that shaft down in the winter they had to thaw the ground before they could lift the dirt out. Then, if you hit permafrost, you had to thaw that, too. Sometimes they just built fires right on top of the ground, waited till it burnt out, then scraped away what melted. Mostly, though, they drove steel points down into the ground with a steam hose

University of Alaska Archives.

Livengood, circa 1930. The Pioneer is the first building you can see on the boardwalk. And the building in the right foreground was a shop built by Eddie Hudson.

attached to it. The miners had a wood fired boiler pumping steam through the points until the section of ground melted and they could shovel it out. Depending on what the ground was made up of they could steam up to twenty feet of shaft a day.

All winter then they hoisted the dirt up and dumped it in a pile to sluice after breakup in the spring. Mostly the work shafts were eight-feet-by-eight-feet or maybe six-feet-by-eight-feet and all the way to bedrock. Naturally the miners wanted to be on shallow ground, less overburden, so they had a shorter shaft to dig. Average around Woodchopper was about a hundred feet. Then they had to crib the work shaft all the way down to keep it from caving in. Once they get to bedrock the ground is froze all the time so they can just dig. But some places they need to crib that too.

Drifting was no picnic. You were hunched over in a tunnel for a couple hundred feet. And you had to work. You had to put out a certain number of wheelbarrow loads. You didn't just put out a couple loads then let John do the work.

They had guys, and this is no lie, they called "leaders". They were some husky big bohunk or Swede that could out work about three ordinary guys. He got four bits a day more and all these other birds would have to try to keep up with him. That's no lie. I was here when that was still happening.

Vincent Tim a cat skinner for Livengood Placers and George Gaddoff, an old timer in front of the Pioneer Pool Hall, 1949. The Pioneer, run by Charlie Erikson had a restaurant, pool table, bar and sold groceries.

Photo by Shade titled, "Winter Sluicing, Howell and Cleveland's Mining Plant, Woodchopper Creek, Alaska". A handwritten note on the photo, probably by Gus Benson said, "old picture taken between Casch [sic] Creek & Sullivan Creek about 1918 and 1920."

Photo titled, "Thawing frozen ground," circa 1910 of a steam point winter mining operation.

In my time mining I don't know of any big cave-ins, but once in Olnes when Fairbanks was just hit, a bunch got trapped. The guys on top knew just where the guys underground were. They took a six inch drill and put a hole down to let them have air and food and candles. At the same time they worked day and night to sink another shaft the hundred feet down. Walter Fisher drilled the relief hole. He told me about it. Everybody was rescued.

A lot of times, too, you'll hit water and your shaft will fill up. Around here in Woodchopper water doesn't come too fast and you generally can pump it out. Some places you hit an underground river and the water boils up. Then you got to get out fast as you can leave your tools and everything. Nothing you can do.

You'd think that miners would get all excited at cleanup, but it's just more work like the rest of it. 'Course there was a little worry about it for the hired workers. Lot of times the crew wouldn't get paid until the spring when they sluiced the dump. They called that "bedrock pay". If you made enough gold, the crew got paid off. If you didn't make enough, you got your room and board and that was it. You was taking a chance. Some places was good and they'd make it. Then a lot didn't and nobody got paid. You went to work with that understanding. If you didn't make it you was out your labor.

When Frank and I first mined that summer in Rampart, we had a lay off Gene Swanson. It was his claim so we paid him 10% of what we took. There was a lot of that what they called "lay men". If the ground was good, a lot of guys made money. And it was good for the owners because they didn't have to do anything but collect money. Generally the royalty was 10 to 15%, lower if the ground was bad, higher if it was good.

The next winter Frank and I did prospecting on Troublesome and Quail Creek. Trapping and prospecting, sinking holes, but we didn't find anything. I prospected on West Fork but never right in Livengood. One spring I worked for Livengood and Spaul sluicing the dump and I worked on Amy Creek another year.

Miners were pretty honest people. Oh, you hear stories of guys picking in the sluice box before cleanup to beat their royalty, but I never been around it. And I didn't ever hear of anybody locking their doors up or anything. Everything was always open. Around here for years nobody ever fooled around locking their doors.

Before the Elliott Highway went through to Livengood, there were only two cars in town. Bob something, I forget his last name, was a wireless operator for the Army Signal Corps. He had a Model T Ford flown in part by part. He put it together to run around on the five miles of road. Another guy Luther Hess was the banker in Livengood and owned a lot of ground. He had a Chevrolet.

When you weren't working in those camps there wasn't much to do. Mining, prospecting, or trapping was the main conversation. Then we might play a little cards or wash our own clothes. If there was fishing close by, you went for that. In the fall we might go off and hunt.

When I first came here people stayed all the time in the country. In the

Stanley Dayo.

Curt Madison.

"Archie Pringle of the Rhode Island Creek out here when he was nozzling with the giant about 1948. That's one of the Beyer's kids with him"

Jimmy Dart at Boulder Creek with a giant, 1984.

winter after they get a grubstake, they go sink holes, prospecting. Or they'd cut cordwood to sell to the drift miners. The town had to have lots of wood too. Everything in the mine was run by steam, the points and hoist. They used hundreds of cords in each place. In late years you had to go way back away from Livengood to get wood. Woodchopper was the same way. You had to go several miles from town for firewood. They cut all the spruce and birch down to three or four inches through.

Before the road it was hard to get supplies into Livengood. They'd either freight them overland from the railroad at Dunbar or bring them up the Tolovana River. Coming up the Tolovana there was a big log jam in one place. They had a tram to get around it. Stuff was reloaded upstream on another boat and floated to about ten miles from Livengood. From Terminal they had a 1919 Dodge with wide rims running on a railroad laid on 2 x 6's. The truck pulled two or three little trailers with the freight. But most of the stuff came in the winter from Dunbar.

In later years Maxi Miller from Fairbanks, freighted in there with a thirty horse gas Cat. That's about the time Livengood Placer bought up a lot of that ground and figured on bringing in a dredge. They probably had a lot of pull with politicians and that might have helped to get the road built.

When the road got in pretty good shape more people in Livengood got their own cars. People from Fairbanks started

Stanley Dayo Collection.

"Me on Kalarney Creek still working at mining, 1979."

traveling back and forth. When miners wanted stuff or parts, they could drive in and get the part right away.

When World War II came along the government shut down all the mines and bought the equipment for building airfields and that. They had a big scare the Japs were going to move into Alaska. They built the Alcan the same time. That stopped a lot of miners for good. Then all the young guys, of course, they slapped in the army.

Before cats and draglines came into this country, everybody who wasn't drifting was hydraulicing. With Cats they strip the overburden off and don't even touch it with water until they get to the pay above bedrock. Hydraulicing was strictly a water proposition. You had to dam creeks at the head and lead them through ditches to your pipeline. The pipe ended in a giant aimed at the face of the cut. All day you played that water over the frozen muck to wash it out. All that mud had to go somewhere and that's why people don't want you to do that anymore. Some people say it kills the fish, but look how silty the Tanana River is and fish live in it.

Now they have slickplates and big boxes with water and riffles. They use pumps to recirculate their water and settling ponds to get rid of the mud. Mining is no gravy train. Lot of years you can lose money. If you get a bum spot or too many breakdowns. Like farming, you get dry years and you lose your crop. Same in mining, in a real dry year you can't sluice. Of couse, if you get in good money and everything goes right, you come out at the end of the season smelling like a rose. But then you can come out pretty hungry, too.

Stampede For Gold

For a successful mine you got to have the money in the ground first. Then you got to have the money behind you to set up and good judgement to not foul it up. In that situation a hard worker can be a good miner. Then the guy with the next claim up the creek might be just as hard a worker but no money in the ground. He's working for just the chance he'll make something. If he comes out hungry people might say he's not a good miner when he is.

Then a lot of guys got the idea they can make a mine work with a bunch of junk for machinery. On any job, road contractors or what, you can't make money with junk. During the season you have to be mining not repairing tractors. Got to keep the dirt moving. Years ago when they mined shallow ground all they invested was a couple sluice boxes, a pick, shovel, and a bag of beans. It's a little different now.

Tommy Hetherington with his refurbished Cat in Manley Hot Springs 1983.

Guys hear stories about this country. They think any creek you go on, if you got a Cat, you'll make money. Well, you can't. First you need good ground. Then there's a million other things; tools, fuel, sluice boxes, welders, cutting outfits, camp equipmment, and money to buy fuel and grub. I knew a lot of stampeders came to the country in '98. Some made money and a lot of them didn't. Some prospected all their lives and never hit nothing. There wasn't a rich creek for everyone that come to Alaska, you know.

When the Klondike was hit in Canada, they went wild in the States. Spreading news around that you could practically kick a spruce tree and the nuggets was hitting you on the head. Thousands of guys came into the country. Not too many made it. 'Course when all the creeks around the Klondike got staked, they started spreading around striking these other camps like Ruby and Iditarod. Guys hit this Tofty country coming from Rampart. But the first ones to get here came from Baker Creek to Eureka, a bunch from back east called the "Boston Boys". Some oldtimers told me that the next spring they found these Boston Boys holed up and all scurvy. They had a tough time making it through the winter.

The stampede is still going on. Few years back a couple guys came in to Manley. Sorry looking characters. One had a bag. The other had a suitcase and a rifle in a scabbard. I don't know where they came from. They stopped me and asked, "How far is it to Eureka?" They heard about how good that country was. I told them how to follow the road.

"We're going out there," he said. "We're going to try to make it. We got fifteen days."

"Well, I wish you luck. I been here thirty years looking for it and I ain't found nothing." He looked at me like I was nuts. Yeah, they're going to find it in two weeks.

When I first came here you could only stake one claim a month, but you could get power-of-attorney from another guy, stake for him and buy him out later. We'd go out on the last day of the month so we could stake another claim the next day. When the State took over recording there was no limit on how many claims you could stake. If you went out with a big crew and a helicopter you could stake quite a few.

Miners generally help each other out like if your tractor is stuck or you need parts. It's nothing like competition. Even with water on a long creek. You have to turn the water back into the creek so the guy below you can use it. There's really no way you can take water away from the other miners. They made that law because I guess years ago they used to have trouble on that.

Most outfits are looking for gold around here, but not all of them. Silver or tin, tungsten, platinum and uranium. Anything in big enough quantity to make it worthwhile. Then a lot of big companies are looking for oil and that's altogether different prospecting.

There were a lot of miners in Manley but then a lot of guys weren't even interested in mining. They come up to cut wood or trap or work on the Road Commission. Lot of guys never put a pick in the ground. Like any game there's shysters involved if it's rich enough. Some guy might move your stakes back in order to get a fraction for himself. And there was guys try to get in someplace to block another guy off and make him buy them out. That wasn't just Alaska. That sort of thing happened all over the world. You get careless, don't stake enough ground and a guy gets

The 1983 Manley Road Crew, Charlie Pearson, Darrel Scott, Dennis Hollingsworth.

below you so you have to have his claim to pile your tailings.

Lot of prospectors never wanted to mine the ground. They find something and sell out. Shorty Barker was lucky four or five times that way. On the other hand, Frank Manley wasn't a prospector at all. He'd go where some guy found a good creek and make him an offer. Then he'd lease it out to a miner. The FE Company had a dredge on some of his ground in Fairbanks. He got a lot of money out of that. He had trouble with partners, too, but they say his word was good as gold.

He was a plunger. If it looked good to him, he went for it. I know one guy said when Manley bought Glenn Creek in Eureka, he rode his horse out to the creek to see it. It looked good to him so he asked the guy how much he wanted for it. The guy said forty thousand. Manley just reached into his saddlebags and pulled it out right on the spot. Johnny Wheel was there. No paper to sign or nothing he said. Manley hired a crew to work the ground and they say that year he made his original forty thousand back and forty thousand more in profit.

Curt Madison.

Old cable drill rig for prospecting at Sullivan Creek on the Tofty Road, 1982.

Chapter Three: Old Manley

Just Looking Around

I had enough money so I quit the road job in Livengood and walked into Fairbanks. In Fairbanks I met Harry Ginrich and Charlie Baker. We decided to walk back to Livengood together. That was June of 1934.

We hung around Livengood for a while because I was pretty well acquainted with the people there. Then Charlie wanted to go in the hills and prospect. He was a hard rock miner. I said I don't know nothing about hard rock. In fact, I didn't know a helluva lot about placer, either. My brother and I worked all summer in Rampart and didn't make no money. One of them deals.

Anyway he said, "What about Sawtooth?"

I knew that country. We trapped there all winter. So I said, "Let's go!" I knew where all the cabins were and the trails. I was pretty well on my toes then.

We was just going to go to the Sawtooths. He thought that would be a good place for a hard rock mine. There was an old cabin there on Buckeye Creek to stay in. After a few days I said, "Let's go over to Quail Creek. That's ten miles from here. Red Anderson, Eddie Farrel, Jack Elliot, and Iver Olsen are mining there." That was just a hop. I was only twenty years old. I could make that in nothing flat.

We got over to where those guys were mining and stayed overnight. They asked us, "What are you going to do?"

"Well, we don't know what we're going to do. We're just looking around."

Then I'd been telling them about the Hoot, so Charlie says, "Let's go over to the Hutlinana."

So we took over to the Hoot. Head of Caribou Creek there was another cabin. When we got there we looked around awhile and came down another eight miles to the hot springs. Me and this American Creek Shorty had been there the winter before. That was as far as I had been down this way towards Manley.

At the Hutlinana hot springs was a real good cabin built by Pete Johnson. You know this Louie Johnson mining in Eureka now? That's his uncle. Anyway there was a good trail from there about ten miles to Eureka, so I said, "Let's go down to Eureka."

"Alright," they said. We didn't much care where we were going.

We get just about to where the bridge is across the Hoot now and here comes a guy out of the brush. He'd been fishing up the creek and when he hit the trail he never even looked behind him. I put on the steam to catch up. When I got close, I let out a whoop, "Hey!"

He jumped around kind of startled. "I didn't think there was anybody within fifty miles of here!" His name was Art Krueger and he was working for Jones right about where Jules Wright has his stuff now. They were shut down on account of no water.

"How far is it to Eureka?" we ask him. He tells us three or four miles. "We're not going anywhere in particular, but we're headed for Manley."

"Well, come on with me to Eureka. I'm staying

"1934, the second year I was trapping."

39

in an old roadhouse. You can stay with me.''

So we went and stayed with him for a few days. We had our own grub, but nothing doing, we had to eat his grub. One of them deals. He took us all around and showed us the mines. Pretty nice old guy.

In fact we went up on Eureka Creek and sniped a bit. A guy by the name of Ed Warshbacher had the creek. Erik Bergman gave us a rocker and we made a couple of dollars goofing around rocking. Then we said to hell with it and we walked in to Manley. That's how I landed here and I never left.

We were staying in the old Pioneer Hotel on the slough. You can see it in some of those old pictures. Then American Creek was starting up their

Looking south across the slough at Hot Springs August 3, 1919. "On the left is the N.C. warehouse that used a windmill for pumping water. The two story building in the center with balcony and porch is the Pioneer Roadhouse that Morris Hildebrake tore down about '36. He used a lot of the wood in that cabin Bob Lee has in the brush. To the right of that with the sign on it was the horse barn when I moved here in the '30's."

dredge so Charlie and Leo walked over there to get jobs.

I fooled around here working for Tim Willard on his fox farm. That place was on the other side of the road from where the school is now and closer to the store.

In the 20's was when trappers really made big money. About '25 to '29 through there. When the depression hit, the bottom went out of the fur market. Fur was so high before that people were starting fur farms. Foxes were worth a lot of money. Guys would go find fox dens in the spring when they were having their young and dig them out. They sold them to fur farmers who raised them.

"The building to the left of the flag was the marshall's office but they took him out of here before I came. To the right of the flag was the schoolhouse which was right between the slough and the house I have now. I tore it down after the flood wrecked it in the 50's. That big round one was a silo they used for silage and corn feed for the cows and horses. To the right of that was a blacksmith shop. It's all torn down now."

There was both a fox farm and a mink ranch here in Manley. Morrison had the fox farm then he sold it to Tim Willard. He raised blue foxes he got off the Chain. See, some big fur outfit leased whole islands on the Chain from the government. They planted these blue foxes on them and didn't have to do nothing for them. They rustled for themselves. There was all kinds of feed down there. Ducks and geese, fish that washed ashore, and mussels. Foxes would get seagull's and shag's eggs.

Every year the company hired a bunch of trappers out of Dutch Harbor to harvest the foxes. They'd wait until the fur was prime and haul these guys over in a boat. For six or seven weeks they trapped out of tar paper shacks. They were getting paid by the pelt and they could get up to 800 fox off one island. After they got so much they'd quit. Every year they kept coming back. No trouble. Didn't have to do a thing, just trap them. Guys like Tim here with foxes in pens had nothing but trouble.

I worked with Tim for awhile when I first came here. You got to take good care of the foxes. You can't just throw them a piece of meat and forget about it because then they don't breed. You got to have certain feed for them. Change the mix at different times and cook for them. Then worm medicine and watch for distemper. Dogs had distemper once in awhile but if it got in your pens it would wipe you out.

Then mating and stuff. You had to be right there. They were a lot of trouble. They get excited fast and like if they got scared when they were having their young they might go and kill all of them. Mink were bad on that too.

Luke Isaacson had a mink ranch where Hubbard lives now. It was no gravy train. You could lose everything easy. But then some of them made out pretty good. Especially these guys buying baby foxes from trappers. Lot of farms starting up all over the country and they got big money for mating pairs. He could get a thousand dollars for a silver or black fox live.

I don't think I'd want to be a fur farmer. Too much trouble. I'd rather be a trapper. When I first came here it was mostly fox and lynx, mink, rats and wolves, beaver. There were quite a few wolves around. Every trapper could get a few of them. Hides were only worth six or seven dollars just like wolverine, but there was a bounty. Guys dug 'em out of the dens in the spring and still got twenty bucks apiece for the pups.

Then I went fishing with Ira Weisner upriver. Fooling around. That winter I trapped out of here around Dugan Creek and across the river. Not too much fur that winter but I made enough to get by. A wood contract came up that year too. Louie Johnson got it. All the steam boats needed

Tim Willard at his fox farm in 1940. "Morrison had the place first raising silver fox. He went out of business and in 1925 Tim Willard came here and started raising blue foxes with a pair he bought from the Aleutian Islands. He just used those dogs to go along the trails snaring rabbits to feed his foxes. He didn't need a whole bunch of dogs just to pull him and his rabbits."

wood so they let contracts for a pile every twenty to thirty miles along the river.

We cut a hundred cords of wood across the river from Baker Creek for eight dollars a cord. And there was snow. Snow up to your ears. You'd fall a tree and you couldn't hardly find it. We'd go out every day for six or seven hours a day. Both of us were pretty young. He was a big *skookum* Swede. We got Mel Maul at the sawmill to pull the wood out to the bank with his Fordson tractor. It had a track on it. We gave him a dollar and a half a cord and helped him load and unload.

I always did a lot of walking. I was going someplace all the time. Just take off with a little grub, rifle, and fish line. I walked in the winter quite a bit, too. I used to keep going all the time. I just like to beat around in the hills. Go out prospecting and, of course, trapping.

When I walked down here from Fairbanks my brother Frank stayed behind. He got on surveying homesteads along the Richardson Highway. The head surveyor was Leonard Berlin, an old hand around the country. During the war he was a big wheel for the Seabee's in Umiat prospecting for oil. After the war he came down here and surveyed a homesite for the N.C. and a 160 acre homestead right at the base of Baker Bluff for old Titus Alexander.

Titus Alexander was the old chief of these guys around here. I knew him, well. He was an old time Indian. All he ever done was fished in the summer and trapped in the winter.

There were guys all the time would get lost or die out in the woods. One or two up the Zitziana never came back. And Titus Alexander, they found him. He had a stroke up the Cosna River and couldn't make it out. He swallowed the barrel, you know, committed suicide. Another guy, Camel went up towards Garnet Creek prospecting and they never found him.

Frank worked the survey that summer of 1934 and stayed the winter in Fairbanks cutting cordwood for Milo Silage in a big camp. Next spring he came down with George Black at breakup. Then on we stayed together practically all the time.

Before Manley got started here there was a little town at the mouth of Baker Creek. They just called it Baker. I knew an old timer out at Eureka who told me they used to go right across the flats from Baker to Overland and on through to Tanana. Overland is the place the highway crosses Baker Creek. There used to be a big horse barn where they'd stop and feed their horses. It was still there when I come here, but nobody was using it.

When I first came to Manley there were a lot of people in the area, but they lived out of town. Not many more here then than there is right now. In the winter there might be a few more, but like Woodchopper, Tofty, and Eureka had a lot of people, too. Manley was just for supplies. That's all. Supplies would come in here by boat and all the miners came in for it. Woodchopper and American Creek. There was people all over you know.

And then there was a lot of people living along the river. Trappers, Whites and Natives, come in for their supplies. There was at least a few hundred people depended on this place all the time.

Harry Martin had a store up at the mouth of the Tolovana and a lot of Natives from up Kantishna River bought their stuff from him. Johnny Cam was at Old Minto so all those Natives bought from him. People living closer to Nenana went in there. Downriver some went to Tanana. The trail was always open. Mail carriers had to open it up after a heavy snow and there was lots of other traffic, too. All the main trails were just as hard as this floor.

I imagine there must have been probably three or four hundred people through this area then. Quite a few people. Most of them stayed year-round. Not many went Outside. They stayed here and worked.

Whites and Natives got along real well, but they mostly had their own towns. Livengood never was a Native camp. A few would come around there, maybe work. And a bunch from Rampart trapped up Hess Creek and would come in for supplies with their dogs. But very few Natives lived

Stephen Foster Collection, University of Alaska Archives.

Vachon's Trading Post at Tolovana July 30, 1919.

around there. Rampart on the other hand was mostly all Native. All the towns on the big rivers, Tanana, Rampart, Steven's Village. Practically all Natives with just a few Whites. Around Manley here there were lots of Natives but not living right in town. Lot of them were living in Crossjacket and they fished around Cosna Bluff. Up by Baker Creek there were lot of them, four or five Native families fishing in the summer and then they'd trap there in the winter. By Rock Crossing a lot of them fished, too. There were a lot of Natives around the river them days. Fishing, trapping in the winter, and cutting a little steamboat wood.

Indian dog teams at Vachon's Tolovana Store, circa 1914.

The Natives would go to work in the mines but there were none around here or in Livengood that had their own diggings. Like around Rampart, Woods and Evans all worked in the mines on and off in the summer when they weren't fishing. But they didn't seem to go for it by themselves.

When I first got here the town was just called Hot Springs. Then we started getting mail mixed up with Circle Hot Springs and Hot Springs, Arkansas, so they decided to change the name to Manley Hot Springs.

I don't know if it was the Postmaster or who it was led the rebellion against it. A few of them said Frank Manley was a horse thief deported to Texas and didn't deserve a town named after him. It didn't bother me one bit. I didn't care what they named it. What's the difference? It was a good name. The guy spent more money around here and done more in the early days than anybody. He built a big hotel. Sure it went broke, burnt down, and he got the insurance money. So what? He had owned a lot of mining

46

ground all over here. Eureka, Iditarod and Fairbanks. I myself thought it was all right. The guy had a little credit coming. He was quite an operator all over the country.

Everybody probably wanted it named after themselves. I didn't pay no attention. You just find anyplace everybody would agree on anything and I want to see it.

Flooded

Breakup in '34 was just average, but once in awhile you get flooded out here. It all depends on the ice. It jams downriver and water backs up. Then you got lots of water coming in. But when you ain't got much ice, it don't seem like snow makes much difference. I seen all kinds of years, lots of snow, and no flood. But if it jams for only two or three hours, we get water all around town. Then it'll break loose and two hours later the water's all gone. That's just enough to get everything stirred up around here good.

"That's a family of Natives up here from Crossjacket getting their supplies. Bunch of them in the boats, I knew all of them well, Lee and Jimmy Albert, Willie Folger Jr., Old Willie, and Big Moses." Circa 1948.

Only one year, spring of 1956, I got flooded out of this cabin. It was kind of a fluke. Ice jammed two places on the river and the main current of the Tanana came down the slough. I wasn't here. I was up freighting for Alfred Gazzi, Alaska Freight Lines, from Eagle to Coronation Gulf on the north coast of Canada. They were building the Distant Early Warning Line (DEW Line).

There was five feet of water in town. I had a cabin right behind where my shed is now. I'd just built it the summer before. Water even floated the

"One of those floods in the 60's when the water backed up and went out right away. That's Gus Benson the postmaster, in the boat going over to the airplane that just landed with the mail. That's the N.C. building behind him."

1982 flood in Manley. Ed Crespin and Stanley Dayo pull a boat they used to get from his house to a small patch of dry ground near the Trading Post.

Ice and water over the Manley Tanana River Landing during the 1982 spring flood.

J.L. Woods fish camp at the Landing during the 1982 spring flood.

cabin. Current coming through town took out the old bridge and the only thing that kept my cabin from following the bridge downriver was Louie Anderson's radio antenna. He had a pipe driven in for the ground lead. It was stuck good because the ground was still frozen. My cabin hung up on it. Even so, I lost a lot of stuff and six or seven rifles.

When I came back from working up north, I jacked it up, put a go-devil underneath and dragged it back with my cat. Water did a lot of damage around town. Everybody took quite a beating. All the wood floated away, and houses jacked around. N.C. store had all its stuff under water. Standard Oil was bringing aviation gas in here in barrels and it was all over the country. Quite a mess. And then all the cars were under water and their clutches froze up. You had to tear them all apart.

I've had two or three different cabins right around the same place here. My brother and a couple guys bought one. I tore that one down when it got jack-knifed in the flood. I had another one got kind of old so I ripped it down and burnt it up for firewood. That's all it was good for.

Sternwheeler Delta *docked on the Hot Springs Slough near the Manley Hotel August 14, 1909.*

There used to be a lot of cabins around here, but when this camp started dying they got run down. People finally tore 'em down and burnt 'em for firewood.

Those early days you just went anyplace and built a cabin. You had squatter's rights. There were two homesteads, Mark Sabin's that Cy has now and the hot springs that Chuck Dart has. Anyplace else you just went and built a

Stephen Foster Collection, University of Alaska Archives.

Hot Springs N.C. Store, 1919. Notice the lack of trees on Bean Ridge where the fire went through before the camp was hit.

Photo by Curt Madison.

The N.C. Store in Manley Hot Springs winter 1982.

Barbara Buzby Boyle Collection.

On the porch of the N.C. Store circa 1930. Standig l-r: Ira Weisner, Mort Sabin, Jayson Buzby (N.C. agent), Alan McLeod, unidentified, George Grant Buzby, Esther, Barbara, Betty Jean, Harry E. Buzby, Jenny Tillison, Amonta Hanson, children: Bobby, Stanley, Donald Hanson, unidentified. Front l-r: Harry Swarburg leaning on porch, Hans Tillison kneeling, Archie Pringle sitting with crossed legs. "Harry Swarburg was a soldier here with the wireless. They had a long building right where the park and bridge is now."

cabin. That's all. After the war they came up with all these homesites, headquarter sites and all that stuff.

Old Timers

When I came here a guy named Harry Saunders lived right above the landing. He used to fish and feed dogs for guys here, board them. Then he'd trap up the Zit. Further up you come to a dry slough and an island. This guy, old timer, Bill Aigler used to live there. He cut cordwood for the steamboats. That's where the slough got its name Aigler's (Eggler's) Slough. There's not too many guys know that. Well you can't hardly find the slough it's all filled in, dry. Ain't been any water in it for several years.

It used to be that the smaller boats, like George Black and them, freighting on the river would use that slough for going up stream because it was slow water. See, steamboats used to land right behind Al Hagen's place. That was the landing. When a steamboat would pull in you could see it from town here. You could stand right on the N.C. porch and see the boat unloading.

When the current of the river was on this side there was lots of water in Hot Springs Slough. The steamboats *Alice* and *Nenana* could push barges right up to the N.C. store. The slough wasn't wide enough to turn around so they had to back down the seven miles to the river. In the winter, airplanes used to land right in front of my place. So much cold water came in the slough that the mouth to Karshner Creek was about the end of the hot water. Now there is so little cold water the slough is open through town all winter from the hot water.

Then the river channel started cutting over to the other side and they couldn't get in the mouth any more. Otto Bayless was head of the Road Commission here when they built the road to the new landing. Me, my brother Frank, and Bob Parr moved the warehouse over to the new landing

51

and set it up for them.

Bill Burk was the first one to live down that way toward the river. He cleared the land off and moved some cabins in from up the Kantishna when they started the school here. He and Elvie had a bunch of kids and he had to put them in school. There was nothing there before him. Then Al and Rose bought him out.

Coming from town before you get to Al's place you can see an old runway. Wein had an airfield in there for a couple years, 1956-57. They had a run from Fairbanks all the way to Nulato or someplace. They'd stop here and Tanana and Galena with C-47s. I met the plane out there twice a week and hauled the mail back and forth to town. And I kept the airport open dragging it with my cat when it snowed. It was just freight, passengers and mail. They never refueled or nothing.

At Baker Creek, of course, there was a sawmill and above there a Frenchman by the name of Giroux lived. So they call that bluff Giroux's Bluff.

When Tofty, American Creek, and Woodchopper were first hit they took supplies over on pack horses. The trail went up the hill past the cemetery followed the ridge and dropped into Tofty. When you get over to the granite pit five miles out the Tofty Road you can see the old trail across the valley on the side of the hill. Frank Manley put that road in. The telephone line went through there, too.

No more than where that road comes down and hits the main road was the old Halfway House. About seven miles out of here. There was a couple cabins there that

Stanley Dayo Collection.

Stanley Dayo in front of a cabin used while trapping above Baker Creek in 1936. "An old Frenchman Giroux built it as a storeroom and Ira Weisner fixed it up when he fished there. Giroux and Old Weserlund burned up in a fire in the main cabin before that.

the freighters used to use if they couldn't make it through with loads. By the time I got here nobody used them anymore.

The main freight used to go down the slough to near the mouth where a guy named McCloud lived. They'd go over the hill from there to Tofty and Woodchopper. Even when I was here old Al McCloud had a couple teams of horses down there for freighting. The Road Commission used to do a little work on the trail in the summer to keep it up. When they started using cats the road moved to where it is now. Al moved out to Fairbanks and kept working as a blacksmith for the Road Commission until the welders put all blacksmiths out of business. He lived to be way past 90. Great big *skookum* Irishman.

They called that place McCloud's Ranch. He had a little meadow cleared off and a horsebarn. His wife run the roadhouse and served meals to anybody. They even had a few beds for people that couldn't make it all the way through. But at one time before that when there was a lot of traffic from Tofty there was a big roadhouse there. A guy by the name of Billy Ford had it. Then Skaya out at Woodchopper bought it and used it for a warehouse. Tony Lanning bought it off of him and tore it down for the logs and iron in it. It was a pretty fair sized place. Used to be a lot of winter traffic them days before there was airplanes in here.

The road used to come from Fairbanks to Dunbar and across the flats to Old Minto. Then it came through Tolovana, and on the Fairbanks Trail to here. It kept going through McCloud's Ranch all the way to Nome. That was the regular route. The telephone went that way too.

Soldiers, the Signal Corps, were scattered

Barbara Buzby Boyle

McCloud's Roadhouse near the mouth of Hot Springs Slough circa 1930.

Photo by George Woods. Rita Cottnair Album, University of Alaska Archives.

Rita Cottnair Album, University of Alaska Archives.

Signal Coprs bridge about fifteen miles from here across a narrow lake at 85½ mile between Tolovana and Manley Hot Springs, 1913. Notice the telegraph wires hung under the bridge.

Known as the Grizzly Gang, this quartet of old timers cut practically all the poles used in constructing the telegraph line and thousand of trees while clearing the right-of-way. Circa 1913.

all over to keep the telegraph line trails brushed out and tripods up. They kept that up for quite a while. Then private individuals had it. When I come around here, you could still talk to Nenana, especially in the wintertime. And down to Tanana. It didn't last long, though, and slowly the lines got shorter and shorter. Pretty soon it was only good to Tolovana and Old Minto. Gus Benson had the line out to American Creek. The line to Rampart was kept up the longest.

If you went over to Benson's or someplace to make a call you might pay him four bits or a dollar. But a lot of people had phones in their houses. They paid him about five dollars a month for it.

This road we have to Eureka is the way they used to get supplies for their mines before they had a road to Fairbanks. The Road Commission punched the trail through from Eureka to Hutlitakwa. Then in '53 or '54 Green Construction got the contract to make the trail into a road. The first year, in the best of times, it was four-by-four conditions. Not really passable. It stayed that way for a couple years, then Green finished the job. After the road was done Bill Vemeyer and Jennings Johnson built the bridges at the Hoot and Baker Creek. Before that you just had to catch it when the water was low and ford the stream.

Going down the slough you no more'n leave the end of the airport and you come to Sabin's Slough. Mark Sabin staked out the homestead Cy and Daisy have now. The next slough, a bigger one, was where Elia Radovitch, Billy the Turk, lived. He was a Slav, I think, but nobody could pronounce his last name so they called him Billy the Turk. He used to make a lot of moonshine in that slough.

The next place, Lottie's Point, has a good story. Sarah and Jimmy Albert were fishing down at the mouth of the slough. She and Lottie Justin got all beered up one day and headed down there in canoes. Sarah started ahead and she made it to the camp. Lottie was behind still sucking on the bottle.

By the time she got down to Lottie's Point, a big rain squall came up. I guess it was just a pouring down. Here she was all beered up trying to maneuver her canoe to the shore. Anyway, she tipped over close to shore. Nothing else to do, she came walking back up to town through the brush. There was an old cabin right where I'm living now and my brother was here. Jesus Christ! Eleven o'clock and somebody's pounding on his door!

"Who is it?" he hollers. It's Lottie. Pouring down rain, she looks like a drowned rat.

"Can I stay here?" she asks.

"Sure," he says, "there's another bed." We had two or three beds in there. All wet, she peeled off and crawled in bed.

So the next day the storm cleared and it was nice. Frank had this inboard motor boat and Lottie had one of these little ratting canoes. She

"Billy the Turk" Elia Radovitch, circa 1928.

asked him to take her down to find her canoe.

"I had a bottle of Seven Crown and seven silver dollars," Lottie told him. There was a lot of silver around here then.

"Forget about that," he said. The slough's pretty wide. He figured there was no way she even knew where she was.

"I know where I tipped over," she said straight out. It was so funny he just laughed that off. "I'll tell you where to slow up."

They get up to the point and Frank cut this old inboard right down slow as he can go. Lottie's out on the bow deck staring into the water. It was so damn funny you wouldn't believe it.

"Stop!" All of a sudden she waves her arm.

Frank threwed it into reverse and stopped. And here's that bottle of booze!

They never found the silver dollars, but they fished out the bottle, of course. She knew right where it was. You couldn't hardly believe it.

The story got around and people laughed about it. They started calling it Lottie's Point after that.

Past Lottie's Point is Duck Flats and then you get to Rex's Slough. The old timer Rex Severwright lived straight out from there on the river. His winter trail cut across the head of that slough when he came to town with dogs. He lived in his place on the river there for years and years. From here he went to the Pioneer Home.

Near the mouth of the slough was Horace Robert's fish camp. Well, the river current was on the bluff side before it changed over. Steamboats used to come right up that side. I fished with Rex there one time. Tim Willard had a fish wheel on the bluff at the mouth of the slough, too. Now that's all sandbar in there. Hard to believe the river moved over so far. It's practically a mile across now.

Dan Green was the first guy to have the roadhouse. He built it over here by the N.C. store where Tom Bean is living. Later, in 1925, they moved it to where it is now. Right across the slough from my place he had a meat tunnel into the hill. They had doors on it so it would stay cold a long time. They'd just take their meat in there and hang it up.

When Dan Green's wife died, he quit. He sold the roadhouse to a guy by the name of Dines Windish and his wife. Bob Isaacson was next and then another guy for a short while. I can't even remember his name. Hubbard owned it after him and he sold it to Monroe. Monroe passed it on to Harley Holman and he sold it to Bob Lee. Before that another guy, Bill Richards who had the hot springs, ran it for about a year. It's changed hands quite a few times.

The N.C. store had a windmill for pumping water. They had a big tank in the store and they'd pump it full with the windmill then gravity feed it down for drinking and washing dishes. For hot water they had coils in the stove that circulated to another tank.

Dan Green owner of the Roadhouse and Johnny Peterson who trapped on the Zit. "He never used dogs or anything, he walked. He'd get somebody with a dog team to haul his grub out to the canyon and then he'd operate out of there. Those were my furs, Dan wanted a picture. It's 1939 in front of the Roadhouse where it is now. In 1925 Dan moved it from next to the N.C. Store where Marshes cabin is, the one Bob Lee owns now.

"Supper at the roadhouse around 1943 when Bob and Lois Isaacson owned it." L-r: Ed Erikson, Norm Suckling, Clare Pringle, Gus Benson, Bob and Lois Isaacson, Norm Suckling's wife Ethel Albert, Jim Farrell the N.C. agent, Frank Dayo, Eric Bergman, unidentified.

Used to be that most of the guys that stayed the winter in Manley earned their grubstake during the summer. Then there were guys like me never stayed here much. I'd go out trapping for the winter and come back in the spring.

But mostly over the winter the guys staying here didn't do nothing. They just waited for summer to go back to work. They might cut a little wood for themselves then go visit, party, play cards. They'd have a lot of parties. The roadhouse was open all the time. They'd go over there and play pan or pinochle or have a little poker game. Holidays they'd have big feeds or a dance. Get beered up, you know, of course.

There was always eight or ten pensioners living here. Old timers through with their working days. They raised a garden in the summer and they lived good off of it. Of course, the pension wasn't much, maybe forty to sixty dollars a month. It stretched a little farther than now, but they had to clothe themselves out of that and everything. Lot of them cut their own wood yet. But at that time it didn't take quite so much money. Seems like people didn't live quite so high as they do now. You could get by if you watched the buck. You could buy your groceries and refreshments. Course you couldn't buy much refreshment if you was on a small pension.

Most of the guys living here

Christmas party at the N.C. Store 1928. Only partially identified. Back: 3rd Fred Hanson, 6th Amota Hanson holding Bobby, 8th Dan Green, 9th Tex Browning, 11th Muriel Anderson, 14th Joe Westerlund, 16th Charlie Shade. Front: 3rd Flora Brestlinger, Mrs. Anderson and Irene Anderson, Elsie Green, Bugleot Anderson, Odney Anderson, Alcoyn Anderson, Jessie Westerlund, Johanna and Irene Westerlund, Arnold and Phillip Anderson, the rest unidentified.

worked all the time, even if they didn't work in the winter. If they did go broke, they all had good credit at the roadhouse or the store. When they went to work they'd pay up. If you paid up, you never had to worry about credit in this country. Lot of stores would carry these guys. Course you couldn't give credit to everybody. You had crooks them days just like now who would beat you out of a buck.

Spring of the year work would open up. All the guys would go to work out in the mines or someplace. The Road Commission in Fairbanks would hire a lot of them. Some guys would go gandy-dancing on the railroad. A few would go to the steamboats. Get on as deckhands.

I guess there was nothing here in Manley until gold was discovered in 1905 in Tofty Gulch. I think Sullivan was the first to strike it, but there were several old guys around here looking. Snyder was another one. American Creek was hit about the same time. Then prospectors started spreading around to Boulder Creek and all through there.

A guy by the name of Ness was one of the first miners on American Creek. He is the one that sold out to the bunch from Fairbanks with the dredge. The dredge is still there but it's all dilapidated.

Tofty was pretty well played out as a town by 1934. There were still people there, but Woodchopper was the last of the deep ground. Ground they'd have to sink holes in and drift along the bedrock. Those guys dug all winter piling up the pay dirt to sluice in the spring. Maybe the town got its name from all the thousands of cords of wood they cut to thaw the ground.

Weighing gold at the N.C. Store at Hot Springs when it was run by Norm Suckling.

The Manley Hotel at Hot springs 1919.

When I first came around here gold was just like money. You could go to the N.C. and they'd take it in. They had scales down there. Either you could buy something or they'd bundle it for you and ship it to the mint. Advance you money or grub or whatever you wanted on it. Lot of the mines would pay the men off with gold when they got done sluicing.

The government would let out a contract for hauling mail. The guy who got it generally hired a man or two to help him. When I first came around here the mail came in once a week from Nenana by dogs. Charlie Shade from Nenana had the contract from there to Tanana. He'd usually get to Tolovana on the first day depending on the trail, then get in here the second day. Here he'd hand it over to Andrew Kozevnikoff who took it the rest of the way to Tanana. They'd both rest a day or two and figure on coming back. If the trail ever snowed in you could always count on the mail carrier opening it up for you. Summer, naturally mail came by boat.

It wasn't until the middle of World War Two airplanes started taking over the mail contracts. And dogs kept it up to Rampart after that. Jesse Evans had the last contract with dogs then Lon Brennen took it over with his planes.

I never spent much time on mail myself. I kept contact with a few people, but I didn't write much. But it seems like there's always somebody howling about the mail not making it in. Old Pete Milovitch, out in Woodchopper, we called him Pete Million, said some guys would run out to the trail looking up and down for their mail. Scream bloody murder if it was late and half of them all they got coming is a Sears Catalog. He got quite a kick out of it.

When I first came here there were a lot of log cabins around but they were all old cabins. Most of them built when this camp was hit around 1907. There must have been 3,000 people right in this town at one time, back and forth to the mines. All the ground was opening up. Lots of prospectors and lots of miners. Mines had big crews working. Lots of chances for prospectors then. Lots of country nobody was in. Then there was businessmen, and wood cutters, road builders and trappers.

Some of these business people always want to make Manley into a resort town. I'm not for it myself. I'd rather live in some hick town than have a bunch of people around.

There's been a bathhouse around here since way before my time. Frank Manley had a big olympic size pool before it burned down. By the time I got here, Tex Browning had the springs and he had a good big bathhouse. The pool was about twenty feet long, fourteen feet wide and about four and a half feet deep. One big pool and heated dressing rooms. You could go in there at 70° below and it was just as warm as this cabin. It finally got old and they burned it down. That was when Bob Beyers, Bob Isaacson and me built this little one we have now. Took up a couple days to put it up in the early '50's. Then Chuck did a little remodeling.

People would shut down for Christmas and all, but not for too many holidays. Working people used to just keep on working. When we did quit we'd have big feeds and get boozed up. There was a big hall here and we'd have dances. There was always a few women around. Never was many though. The population of women was a shortage. Lot of men but not too many women around no place. Just wasn't a lot of women around the country them days. Then in later years more of them started coming in.

Photo by Curt Madison.

I didn't go to too many dances myself. I never hung around town much. In the winter I was trapping and I didn't come in too often. I just didn't care about town then. I was young and I wanted to be out. I wanted to trap and run around the hills. There was a

The Dart's hot springs bathhouse 1983.

lot of guys, trappers and prospectors, went out and didn't come in all season. There was no roads or nothing so you wasn't coming in town every week or, like now, with good roads, every night.

Summer was the same way. Guys would go out ten or fifteen miles. Some of them wouldn't come in all summer. You worked hard them days. You had to put in a good shift. You didn't stand around at that time. Everybody had to work.

Those that did come in for the Fourth of July got here the evening of the 3rd. They'd stay the 4th and be back out the evening of the 5th. Might be a few lingering on that got beered up and couldn't make it out.

The airport we have here was nothing but an oat field. It was part of Mark

Sabin's ranch of vegetables and grains at Hot Springs 1919. "When I came here he had a frame house where the store is now. This long building was gone when I came around."

Sabin's homestead. He didn't care. He let the planes land there in the summer. Then when traffic got heavier he made a deal with the Territory and they bought that land off of him. The Road Commission did some work on it clearing brush around the sides. Then one year Cy and I got the contract to extend it. We knocked the brush down and graveled it right to the slough.

It's a pretty good airport now compared to what it used to be. They do a little work on it all the time. This lower end, though, needs to be built up. When we get high water here in the spring at breakup it floods for quite a ways.

Right after the flood in '56 the N.C. Store closed down. The camp was kind of dying down and the mining was kind of going. The price of gold was thirty-five dollars an ounce. There started to be a lot of construction with the army paying higher wages. That's when everybody started pulling out.

For a long time there was a magistrate here, a judge. He'd marry you or fine you or you could bring a case in front of him to settle a big argument. He took care of all the recording of all the mining claims and all that stuff.

He was here all the time, but he didn't get a salary. He got a fee for recording claims and maybe ten dollars for marrying somebody. It was no living. You had to be retired or have another job. Gus Benson was the last magistrate and had the post office, too, so it worked out pretty good for him.

About the oldest guy I know from around here is Einer Anderson. We called him Red. He come around in 1912. Now he's living in Graehl in Fairbanks. He must be past 90. Getting pretty shaky last time I seen him. But the only thing he's got on his mind is going back and prospecting. I visited with him a year or so ago. The first thing he asked me was what was I going to be doing in the summer.

"I don't know for sure," I told him.

"I know a place, " he said, "we got to go back there and sink a hole."
And here he's even stumbling around his own house.

"Yeah,yeah," I humored him, but he was too old. He couldn't do it.

He was quite a goer when I first come to the country. He mined Glenn Creek in Eureka. He sold that, went Outside, and came back to Rampart. He'd been all over Alaska.

John Barrett is another old timer who wouldn't quit. He had the claims up on top of Hot Springs Dome. He was 88 years old walking around with two canes, but he was still climbing up the mountain prospecting in that hard rock. Took him eight hours to walk up the three and a half miles from here. One day he left to go home and never returned. They went looking for him but I think one of his shafts caved in on him or he cut his fuse too short on the dynamite. The shape he was in he couldn't have gotten too far. A storm blew in on his way up and some say he got lost in it. All the placer miners here quit to look for him. Must have been twenty-five to thirty guys looking for him. Since then there have been all kinds of prospecting and surveying parties up there and no one has seen any part of him.

He had a couple hard rock claims and a cabin. You can still see the remains. It was a gold prospect alright and lead and zinc too, but not anything in paying quantities. I used to haul stuff up there in the spring for him. No timber or anything that high. Bull-headed old Irishman.

There were a lot of hunkies, you know, Bohemians and Yugoslavs, in this country. Irish too. Most of them came to the northern states, then came here. There was a lot of foreigners around here.

Chapter Four: Dogs, Hunting, Fishing, Trapping

Out In The Woods

I used dogs all the time after I was here. You just about had to have dogs for trapping and to get your supplies out. Especially when you got back out quite a ways. That first winter in Rampart a guy gave me some dogs and another guy let me use his dogs while he went Outside. He wanted somebody to take care of them. They were old dogs but they were alright. They'd work, you know. Then when I came down to Manley I got some dogs from another fella and raised my own.

Between my brother and me, we had ten or eleven dogs one time, but that's too many. Too hard to feed. Mostly we'd feed cornmeal and fish, game, rabbits, scraps, anything we could get hold of all winter. Spring of the year finally they're easy to feed. You always had beaver meat and lots of lynx around then.

I always had fair-sized dogs because I wasn't racing. Dogs had to work. Had to be able to pull something and be good travelers. Big enough to break through snow, but not too big. Then too small a dog takes too many to pull a load and they eat just as much as a middle-sized dog.

I always used a freight sled with ten or

Stanley Dayo.

"The cabin at Hutlinana Hot Springs when Eric Bergman was trapping there. I took the picture of my brother Frank, Jim Rider and Tom McKennan. That's when we were hauling our drill and stuff up to Caribou, March 1939. That was my freighting sled I bought from Old Willie Folger for twenty-five dollars. That's what they were selling around the country for."

eleven foot basket. We'd either make them or buy them from the Natives. You could get a good one for twenty-five bucks. Making one wasn't hard, you just have to get some good birch and rip it or split it out. Six or seven inches is a big enough tree. Chop into it to test the grain and look for a good straight one.

I fished for my dogs several years on this river while I was trapping. 'Course everybody was doing that then. I tried up here at Baker Bluff, at a bluff down below here, and right across from the landing. It went the same as anything, a lot of good years and some bum years. It all depends on how the run was. One year me, my brother, and Ira Weisner had four fishwheels in and we got just enough to

"1944, Rex Sevewright, an old '98er who had a fish camp on the river where the slough hits the Tanana. His outfit was washed in the river when the bank fell in.

feed our fifteen dogs. No fish that year. We even tried to set two wheels side-by-side, covered pretty near half the river and still there were no fish in the river. We didn't get but about four or five fish in each wheel. Then the next year we had one fishwheel and we got a thousand or two a night. Our raft would be underwater in the morning and fish running out of the box.

A few guys had three-basket wheels but we just used two. Generally my wheels were about ten feet by ten feet. Some guys had twelve foot baskets and some only six foot. It all depended on how hard you wanted to fish. And it depended on the spot. If you got in a good spot all you need was a small wheel. Seems like the fish would hit in it. Some places no matter what you did you never got fish.

A lot of guys used leads in the water next to their wheels. I never put any in because I always caught all the fish I wanted without them. I never wanted too many. You couldn't sell them. Well, there were a few guys around town

Click Bishop and Greg Taylor picking a net near the site of Rex Sevewright's old fish camp, 1981.

Clyde Mayo's fishwheel below Rampart. L-r: Clyde, Roger and Click Bishop, 1983.

with dogs who would buy a few dry fish, but there was no big market for them. That summer of the big run, my brother and I dried a hundred bales in just a little while. It took about thirty fish for maybe fifty to fifty-five pounds to a bale.

Through the winter we figured a pound and a half of fish a day per dog. 'Course you couldn't feed straight fish. Around the home cabin we cooked up cornmeal and oatmeal and threw in a good chunk of tallow.

When there were a lot of fish it didn't pay to fish. I could go to the N.C. store and buy dog salmon five cents a pound. Fish camps would board dogs for a couple bucks a month a dog. For a guy who was fishing for his own dogs and feeding them anyway the extra money was all gravy. See there was a lot of dogs in this country in the 30's. Even guys living out not trapping had a few to haul their wood and come into town. Then there was a lot of big teams for freighting and hauling mail.

Mail carriers had contracts and they were sure of their money, but I still think trappers made out better. It all depends on how trapping is. When there was fur, rabbits and that, trappers make out pretty good. But years when there was no rabbits you didn't do very good. You had to really rustle the country. Trapping all depends on how hard you worked at it. Some guys went out and they sat out in the cabin. They didn't come in it very much. Then a lot of guys that worked at it, when there was fur around they made good catches. They made good money.

It depends on the market, too. Like back when they were allowed to shoot beaver, you only got ten dollars for a big blanket. In the 20's, before I was trapping, fur prices were real good. Then in '30 and '31 it was depression and the price went down. Right after the war prices were low too. Lynx and foxes were worth nothing. They wouldn't even hardly want to buy 'em. A couple dollars for a fox. The style went out. Lynx wasn't worth nothing. You get five, six, ten dollars for a lynx. And it'd have to be a good lynx if you got ten dollars for it, I'll tell you. If you didn't have marten, mink and lots of other fur they wouldn't even buy 'em. If you went in there with nothing but lynx and fox, they wouldn't even buy 'em. I sold lynx as cheap as three dollars apiece. Nothing. The same lynx now they're probably getting 150 or 200 dollars for it.

There were a lot of fur buyers. All the N.C. stores bought fur and Vachon did in Tanana. There was Johnny Sweigler and Charlie Main in Fairbanks. Then there'd be a lot of them traveling around. Leo Kay was another one and old Goldstein from

Photo by Curt Madison.

Joee Redington's split dog salmon, November 1980.

69

Juneau. There was one guy around they used to call the Walrus. He had a big mustache. Every place, every trader in the country that had a store bought fur.

Some guys came in and sold their fur at Christmas, but I usually waited until the spring. Then if there was somebody here could give me a good price I sold the whole thing. Then a lot of times I'd go into Fairbanks where there was more buyers and I had a better chance. You have to shop around to get a good price. If you got took it was your own fault. You didn't have to sell. The only time you could make a mistake is if you sent your fur out. Then they had the fur and they could give you whatever they wanted. You were better off if you could look the guy in the eye and say yes or no.

Sears and Roebuck and West Coast Grocery both would sell your furs for a percentage. You could do good with them. Of course, Seattle Fur Exchange is another one. And Maas and Stephens are an old fur outfit. I shipped them a little now and then and done pretty good. But then there was a lot of gypo outfits around. They come up with a big price on the offer, but guys get stung with them.

They'd have all kinds of excuses for giving you a low price. They'd say the fur was damaged or short hair or the color wasn't right. They'd have two or three grades. You get a big price for one and then the other one wouldn't get half as much for practically the same skin. It was skin game alright.

Protect The Game

My brother and I trapped together quite a few years. Late years he trapped by himself and I did alone, but we'd always trap beaver together every spring. We'd go down on the Tolovana below Livengood in the flats. He'd go one way and I'd go the other. If the trail was tough, we'd go together to break it out. Usually we'd set traps and build the camps together. When we sold the fur we split the expenses and profit right down the line 50/50. You don't figure how much you catch and how much the other guy catches when you're partners.

Now some guys went out together but they'd have separate lines. Couple guys here, Jim Alexander and Tom Armstrong went up the Cosna like that. They go together just for company. Whatever they caught was theirs. If one wanted to lay in the cabin, he stayed. If the other wanted to trap, he trapped. No concern of one another. Of course, it was like everything else, all kinds of squabbles when one guy figured he done more work than the other guy. Might be what you call "cabin fever". Anything you do is wrong. Everything has got to be their way. You just can't please them. Even if you bend over backwards, it's still wrong.

Me and my brother, for years we got along good. We had no troubles. But he wouldn't take another partner. He'd rather trap by himself. When I went on Hess there, I was by myself, too. I only had a partner one year. Frank never had another partner for the simple reason he didn't want to get in no arguments. He said, "It don't bother me to stay out in the woods. I can do anything I want and I ain't got nobody to complain." I was the same way.

A lot of guys can't stay out by themselves. They got to be together. There's a lot of guys like that. But it never bothered me. And it never bothered my brother. When we trapped together, even though we both had dogs, he'd never go into town. Fall of the year he'd go out and not come back in till the spring when trapping was done. I'd make trips and haul out the food. He'd say, "You go in. When I'm going in, I'm going to stay."

Those early days there was only one game warden in Fairbanks, Sam White. He didn't bother you. Fellas didn't abuse the laws too much. 'Course they was all taking a little game. That was common. Sam White knew all that. But guys weren't shooting something just to see it kick or for the horns or something like that. They were chasing a moose or a caribou for something to eat.

For your own use at that time a guy was allowed five caribou. Legal. But you could take all you wanted. If you could eat more, you took 'em. All depends on family men and that. Of course a lot of caribou went for dog feed in them days, too. But there was a lot of caribou when I come around. They'd come through here for days. Some years they'd hang around here all winter. Bunches would be around the North Fork. Last caribou I seen was up near the head of the Hutlinana in 1947. I was mining on Gunnerson Creek. Walking in the woods I seen fifteen in one bunch. After that they never came around. You know how caribou are, they change their migration routes. Same thing on Hess Creek. A lot of them in there one winter and the next winter not any.

Caribou are good and fat in the fall, but you get 'em way in February and they're nothing but a bag of bones. That was a real screwball deal having the hunting season open all year. Sure you can eat them in the winter if you're starving, but 99% of the people shooting them was just after the horns. 'Course if you're out trapping and you got to feed dogs, that's different. A dog will eat anything. It ain't very good feed but it will keep 'em alive, you might say. Having the season open all winter is just plain foolishness. You know most guys out hunting wasn't after feed. Especially so many GI's. They had time. They go out. They all want to shoot caribou. Well, you know what happened. Now there's no caribou.

Trophy hunters come around Manley here now, too. Same as any place they're looking for horns and hides. They want me to take them out, but I'm not interested in that. I had a couple chances to go in with established guides, but I just don't go for waiting on somebody. Lot of hunters are good guys, but some of them are a pain.

They're cracking down on trophy hunters more now. They can't just take the horns and leave the meat, can they? They got to take the whole thing, don't they? They can't leave it any more like they used to. And so much of the game thing now is these small airplanes and sno-gos. Hunters get to all these small lakes with floats and are killing off the game.

Well, I'll tell you the way it looks to me, and I know it. There's so many guys coming up here for work. They all got a car full of guns. And they all want to shoot a moose or a caribou or bear. They come in here in the spring of the year saying, "Where can I get a bear?"

"You ain't going to find one in town," I tell them. "Go out and hunt 'em." You know what I mean? What can I say? There's a lot of game gets killed off that way.

Now look at the army. Most of them guys want to hunt. And most of them don't even need the meat. They're living out there in the base. They've got everything they want to eat. All they want is a set of horns.

Cy came down the road one day from Livengood. It was just getting dark. Here these five GI's just got a moose right off the road. All they wanted was the horns. They asked Cy if he wanted the meat. He had a load of freight so he couldn't take it right then. Nice moose. A car came right behind him with three or four of Sally Hudson's relatives in it.

They stopped and Cy asked them if they wanted a moose. They were hunting anyway. "Sure," they said, and went down and quartered it up. If they didn't come along you know it would have laid there and spoiled.

Another time some guy shot one over here and just took the hind quarters and the head. The rest was laying there. Walt Woods happened to come along just a little bit after that and took the meat home to his family. Otherwise it would have spoiled. There's a lot of that going on.

Then there's a lot of game laws I don't agree with at all. Like banning aerial hunting of wolves. There's all kinds of wolves in the country and there's places that airplanes can't get to 'em. Let the hunters keep 'em down. I'd rather eat a moose than a wolf, you know. That's what it amounts to.

This notion that wolves only get the weak, the old, and the diseased is nothing but a lot of bull. I've seen two year old moose and calves killed, everything. Caribou the same way. They follow the caribou, and every time they want one they'll drag it down. I've found a few moose that just the lungs and nose are ate up. Wolves will go for the heart and liver, tongue, and chew the nose off and leave it. I've found several of them. I set traps around 'em and the wolves never have come back. Traps be there all winter and the wolves never come back because there's lots of game around.

The nature of wolves is they like to hunt. Whenever they get hungry if there's something handy, a pack of them just go get something fresh. Drag it down. That old and weak stuff just ain't true. Do you think a pack of wolves is gonna go and drag down an old skinny moose when there's a nice good fat one? Common sense tells you what will happen.

Some guys are no easier on the country. Just about anything they see they'll kill. Regardless what it is. Rabbits, ducks, birds, or anything. They just want to be shooting something. Only thing you can do is turn him in. Some guys are just bloodthirsty. They'll even go around shooting these grouse when they're mating, going to have their young and that. Like to see something just to shoot it. That's one thing about the law, it keeps guys like that down a little bit. They're scared.

And some guys shoot ptarmigan in the middle of the winter. Sure if you're absolutely hungry and will eat anything, go ahead. But to eat one of those dried up scroungy birds! There's nothing to them! Why shoot 'em? You let them go and there'll just be that many more come summer. They breed up.

If a guy don't protect the game himself, you know what's going to happen. There won't be any. When I was trapping marten, I'd just take so many and I'd quit. Then I'd go back every year and do the same. Get the same amount of fur. It's a little bit different with lynx because they move. When there's no rabbits, there's no lynx. But marten live on small game and they hang around the same area. Beaver are the same way.

When my brother and I were trapping we'd take one or two big beaver out of every house and quit. Every year we could go back and do the same. We could get our limit with no problem. But if you go and camp right by a hole and get 'em all, young ones and big ones. What's there? Nothing.

You can wipe anything out. If you go early and stay late trapping marten, you go back the next year and there'll be nothing. Same for foxes. Hang around an area, stay there and trap late and you can clean 'em out pretty good. No, the trapper has to watch that.

That's the reason in Canada they have these registered lines. Guys would be for years on them lines and they took care of it because that was their living. Nobody else could go on there.

These guys with airplanes are pretty bad for getting on somebody's line. I know trappers around Lake Minchumina trapping beaver and airplanes land right on their lakes. One guy finally just quit trapping. He was doing like we used to do, take a couple big ones and leave the others to breed up. Here some pilot came in after he left and trapped the houses clean using the same holes in the ice! Now if that ain't something!

What're you going to do? There's no law says he can't do that. The only thing is that if you're a better man, you go and knock his can off. Game Commission will just say he has as much right to trap those beaver as you do. This state should have had registered traplines for years. Trappers have wanted them but they won't bring any law for it into effect.

The Alaska Department of Fish and Game started an antlerless season for moose around here in fall of '63. We had a petition out to try to stop it. They just ignored our petition. They never done a thing until now there's no moose. A few years ago they come around and interviewed me. They said, "What do you think about closing the season altogether?"

"Might as well." I said, "There's no moose anyway."

Stanley Dayo.

"1938 or '39 at my trapping cabin on the West Fork of the Tolovana by the cold springs. That's when you could hunt beaver. Ten dollars a blanket was all you could get."

75

So they took the antlerless season off fall of '74 and closed the season down to fifteen days from thirty. There were just too many hunters. Sundays, holidays, and weekends. The dust wouldn't hardly settle from one car and there'd be another one.

Bears

I've lived out in the woods all my life ever since I was just a kid, and a lot of these Jack London type stories are just made up. They're just blown up to sell a story. The public is gullible, they'll buy anything. Like wolves, they're not dangerous. Bears are the worst. A lot of guys have been attacked by bears. One guy right over here, Harry Rider...well, the dogs brought the bear to him, too. By the time he could get his gun off the packboard, the bear mauled him. He lay there two or three days unconscious at the mouth of the Steward River. The pilot of a steamboat going to Dawson saw the dogs milling around on the bank and pulled in. That's the only thing that saved him. He got to the hospital in Dawson and eventually pulled through. He lived right where Neubauers live now.

One time I drove my dogs from the head of the Hoot, dropped into Quail Creek and over to Troublesome. It was forty below as I crossed the Sawtooths and pulled up to my headquarters on West Fork. A hard day breaking out a foot of snow on the trail. It was way past dark. A bear had been in there. He tore ten feet of the roof off and demolished the insides. You'd think somebody had been in there with a splitting maul. I had the stove pipe leaning up in the corner. He had that flattened out and scattered around. Poles from the bed were everywhere. Canvas on the walls were ripped down and the tables were smashed. The window was broken out and the door was gone. Shelves were ripped up. He chewed a couple cans of Blazo and threw the gas light out in the yard. Frank found it the next spring.

Pretty disgusting. But what can you do? I just dug in to fix it. I threw the sled tarp over the roof and nailed some poles in the window hole. Somehow the stove pipe got pounded back out enough to fit it together and I got a fire in the stove. It had to be a big brownie.

Another time I was working for McGee out in Tofty. It was the spring of the year and the road was washed out. I had to walk into Manley to get a Cat part. While I was gone and Sil Kozloski and Teddy Luke were about a mile from the cabin stripping ground, a bear got into our place and tore everything up. That night Sil, went back to the cabin to cook something to eat. Twelve midnight but it was spring of the year and still plenty light yet. Here the bear came back to the cabin while he was in it. I had two rifles out there but Teddy had one in his place a little ways away and I took the other one with me to town. Sil had no gun. The bear was trying to get in the cabin after him. He kept beating on dish pans and frying pans and hollering. Finally he run the bear off.

I stayed overnight in Manley and come back the next day with my dog, a labrador retriever, half labrador and half bird dog. Real good dog for bears. We were talking about this bear. Sil said be ready because he'll be back. So I had my gun by the head of the bed with a shell in it. I was sleeping by the door. There was a low window in the wall.

As soon as the bear came to the cabin the dog let me know. He jumped up and started whimpering. He didn't bark. I jumped out of bed but the bear was looking in the low window and run off. I chased out the door. We wanted to get rid of the bear 'cause we was gone so much from the cabin we figured he'd get back in again.

The bear was running straight away from me and I took a shot at him. I hit him but I didn't kill him. Then I don't know what happened. Might be he didn't know what he was doing or...he turned around and come right back towards me at full speed. 'Course I nailed him again. The second shot killed him.

Then that same year it happened again. We were working at the head of the ditch by an old cabin. Another guy had left earlier and left a bunch of grub in the cabin, canned fruit and flour. Bears got in and chewed up these cans and stuff. Everytime you'd go up there you'd have to have a rifle. There was a lot of bears that year. They killed thirty some around here. Well, that was the year the bear killed Bill Strandberg at his mine.

Anyway this particular day we was working up the cut, me and a guy running a backhoe. We was working on the ditch and I was driving the Cat. I had my rifle with me all the time because we'd have to walk about a mile and a half to camp. That one morning we were coming back from work and his dog, a malemute run ahead towards the cabin right away. We figured there was something in the cabin. We get up on top of this ditch bank and pretty soon this dog came running around the end of the cabin with this big brown bear after him. After he come so far the bear turned and run back around the cabin. When he done that the dog run back after the bear. Then the bear started after the dog again. Naturally the dog headed straight for me and this other guy. Right full bore. It's really funny. The dog is running full blast and this bear is about a foot behind him with his mouth wide open trying to grab him. I got my rifle on ready and when they come over the bank of the ditch we was right there. It wasn't over twenty-five or thirty feet so I nailed him. I got him right through the neck and killed him dead on the first shot.

We would have had something on our hands there with that brown bear. I told this other guy, "If we didn't have a gun, I bet I could have outrun you to the camp."

He was a good sized brownie but he was in poor shape. It was probably in late May, or June I'd say. They'd been out of the hole for quite a while. There was bears all over town that year, 1963. Walter Woods shot one right in his yard. It come right after him. They were crazy. I don't know what was the matter with them. All poor, hungry. All in bum shape. They were just skinny. They couldn't get nothing to eat. You could play a tune on their ribs.

Nothing but bone and hide.

That was an odd year. I've seen lots of bears in my time. Most generally you make a noise, especially with black bears, if you didn't surprise them, they take off. But that year they'd come after you instead.

Bill Strandberg and his brother Harold were mining together in Tofty right next to where I was working for McGee. Bill left to work on some rigging, machinery, on the Koyukuk. They had some property yet on Indian River near Hughes. He went up there to do something just a few days. When he come back, he was in Manley here.

We picked him up in McGee's car and took him to his camp in Tofty Gulch. Kind of fall of the year and it was getting dark already. About ten o'clock at night it was pretty dusky. No one knew it but apparently a bear had gotten into his mess hall when he was gone.

McGee and I left him at a cabin alongside the road. The one Greg Gau uses for his trapping cabin. We turned around and went back to McGee's where the Tofty camp is now.

McGee has some other property on Porcupine Creek in Circle country out of Miller House. The next morning we went out there to pick up some stuff. I drove one truck and he drove the other one. Dixie was still a little girl staying in Manley with Judy Woods. I picked her up and took her along for the ride to Miller House.

In the meantime, that night Bill stayed in his cabin fine. Next morning he went over to the cook shack where the bear been in there raising hell and he started cleaning up the mess. Then the bear come back again and got him. Dragged him out and had his body laying under a truck. Harold came out from Manley to see how Bill was doing. He drove as far as Blowback where the road was washed out. He walked from there and found Bill killed. So he went to McGee's camp and told Sil and Teddy Luke.

They took my .270 and they had their own .30-'06. 'Course Bill was all dead, but they figured the bear might come back because he had been eating off of Bill's body. Well, the bear did come back and they shot him.

The night before it rained heavy and washed out all the roads around here. Coming back we got stuck in Livengood and stayed there overnight. It came over the radio that a bear killed Bill Strandberg.

Next day the road at Hutlitakwa was washed out. The Road Commission fixed it and we got to Eureka. All that road was washed out in the bend where McMullens are now. Me and Dixie had to sleep in the pick-up over night till they come from this end and fixed the washout.

Another time I was fishing at the landing one year with Jerry Saunders. I went out early one morning to get the fires started in the smokehouse. We had this long smokehouse. It took a couple fires to get the smoke all around. I had the fires started and chopped some wood for later in the day. I went back in the smokehouse with an armload of wood and here a bear was in there knocking fish off the rack left and right. I ran back to the cabin to get my gun and get rid of him, but he was gone by the time I got back.

Jerry had a couple loose dogs around. They let us know there was something around that evening. "I'm going to go out the trail, Jerry. I might run onto the bear and I can get rid of him," I told him. "He'll get into the smokehouse tonight while we're sleeping and he'll fix it good."

I put a shell in the barrel of my .25 high power rifle and started walking down Jerry's trapping trail. There's all kinds of high bush cranberries growing over the trail. Dense, you could hardly see the ground. I wasn't five feet from that bear when he jumped up in the trail. I walked right onto him. But I had my rifle. Shell in the barrel and everything. I swung right around and touched one off. Got him right through the neck and killed him. I don't know what he would've done, no chance to find out.

Stanley Dayo.

"That's Dixie when she was a little girl next to the Old Chevy around 1960."

The only time I put a shell in the barrel of a gun is if I see something or I know something is right close. Otherwise I never do. I always got plenty of time to get one in. I never leave a shell in the chamber. I know a lot of guys shot themselves that way. They told me themselves. They're carrying the gun and it gets hooked up on some brush or something. Goes off into their leg.

Seems there are always bears around fish camps. Alex Seaholm trapped and fished about fifteen miles below town here. He had a bear stealing fish out of his smokehouse, so he set out some guts and dried fish and laid for him with his rifle. He waited and waited until finally he fell asleep. While he was sitting there, the bear came and dragged off a whole bale of dry fish! Fifty pounds to the bale, you know. After that the bear never showed up again.

Alex was quite a man, but he had a knack of just missing it. When he first got to Alaska, he and four other guys were stampeding into Nome. They landed on the beach and took off into the hills to make their fortune in gold. For two or three months they prospected around, but never found a trace. In the meantime back in Nome, other stampeders found the richest strike yet right on the beach. When Alex got back to Nome there were tents all over the beach where he and his buddies camped. He quit looking for gold right then. Here he was sitting on top of a million dollars and walked away from it. He trapped here until he got too old, then moved down to Tanana. From there he went to the Pioneer Home.

Wolverine

Wolverines are bad for getting in cabins, like if you got meat cached or something. They're bad on that. 'Course they'll follow your line and pick up fur for you. Tear it up and eat it. They're good on that.

I've had them get a little fur on me, but most generally I make a lot of trail sets with big traps and get them before they can run my line. I put traps close to marten sets, but it's hard to judge a wolverine. They can do anything.

The first year I was trapping up Hess, Jim Pickings went in with me to set up the line. Just getting started in the fall, he stayed out to hunt moose and I walked the forty miles into Livengood to get some grub.

I got back four or five days later and Jim had gotten a moose. A small moose, he said it was about 400 pounds. He made a rough cache in a tree and put the meat up. That night when he was walking back to the camp, he saw this wolverine running across the flat right near the moose.

First thing he said to me was, "Let's go cache that moose better so the wolverines don't get it." It didn't help. This was five days later and the wolverines had all the meat off the cache and on the ground. Just bones laying around, cleaned up slick.

Later I was coming up Hess Creek one time and about a half a mile before my cabin I see where this wolverine hit my trail. He turned and headed right for the cabin. Well, I know what I'm going to see. I was gone a week from the cabin and there was no door. I just hung a canvas up for the door. And the trip before that I left a bale of fish in there for my dogs. I had five dogs that year. 'Course when I seen this track on fresh snow, I was thinking he got in the cabin and tore up all the fish.

I pulled up to the cabin and his tracks went right past, not six feet from the door! He headed up the creek following my trail. It was early afternoon so I unhooked the dogs, put on my snowshoes, and headed up after him. That wolverine walked right into a big number four I had set in the trail. Ten feet farther on I had a marten in a cubby. Apparently he smelled the marten and wanted him worse than the dried up dog fish.

Another year I set out early in October to Hess to straighten things up before the season opened. I went in about twenty-five miles on a couple inches of snow. I was using four dogs that year. I had some fish for dog feed and my own grub, a couple rifles. Right by the cabin were a bunch of big trees and I had houses for each of the dogs.

The dogs woke me up about three o'clock in the morning raising Cain. There was a lot of moose around so I figured one wandered in the yard. Then all at once they quit. It was dark so I didn't pay any attention. The next morning I got up, started a fire, and went outside to get some water from the creek.

I heard some noise so I looked off in the willows for a moose. Suddenly here's this wolverine backing down a tree! What happened, that night the wolverine came to the cabin and walked right between the dogs. When they started barking he ran up the tree.

By the time I got in the cabin and came back with my rifle, he was headed into the brush. I touched one off, but I missed him. That winter I caught three around there anyway, so I think I nailed him.

The same winter I made a run over my whole line and ended up at a line cabin ten miles away from the first one. I picked up about twenty-five marten and skinned them all out right there. I took all the carcasses and piled them outside the cabin. If I ran out of dog feed I could cook them up with cornmeal and dogs will eat it.

I left for a week and it snowed a foot while I was gone. A wolverine come to the cabin and packed all those carcasses off. On top of that I had a brand new pair of snowshoes leaning up against the cabin and he swiped one of them. I looked all around there, but so much snow I couldn't track him. What got me, he left that one snowshoe.

Those wolverines can really be destructive. I've had 'em get into my caches and destroy a good Woods Three Star sleeping bag, tent, and all kinds of stuff. Finally I got wise to wolverines and bears both. The best cache you can make for anything is get a heavy wire or cable, string it between two trees, and hang your stuff out in the middle. I make it plenty high off the ground and throw a canvas over it to keep it dry. I came back to one of those caches after two years. Bark was ripped off the trees where animals tried to get in, but nothing could.

You hear all kinds of stories about wolverines. You pick up books about trappers and they say they trap all their life and only catch one wolverine. That's just a bunch of bull. Wolverine is the easiest thing to catch. They'll walk into just about anything. All you got to do is tie a chunk of hide or something to a tree and set a bunch of traps around. They'll plow right into it. Only time they get a little smart is if you nip one. When he loses his toes in a trap he'll be cagey. Wolves and coyotes are way harder to trap.

I've never seen yet where any wolverine got on my line I couldn't catch 'em right away. 'Course there never was very many around. The best I did was seven one winter. Then I only got six or seven dollars apiece for them. That was all they were worth. That plus the fifteen dollar bounty. Other fur was worth more. A good lynx was fifty dollars and marten were forty to forty-five dollars. Red fox were only fifteen dollars, but cross-fox went up to forty dollars and a silver would get seventy-five dollars.

Moose

There were a lot of moose around Hess Creek. We never had any trouble getting meat for the winter. So many that in rutting season, you never know, any little noise and they might come after you. That same year Jim Pickings and I were on Hess we had a run-in with one.

I went to town again and bought a lot of grub. It was too much to pack so I got Lon Brennon to freight it out with his airplane. Jim marked a target and I kicked the sacks and boxes out the door of the plane. We dropped food, traps, and all kinds of stuff.

That morning Jim went over to gather up the drops and for some reason he packed his rifle along. It wasn't over a hundred yards from the cabin and he couldn't tell me why he bothered to carry the gun. We had two dogs with us, too, but we just let them run free. Good dogs, they stayed right close by. All of a sudden one dog takes off into the brush. Jim said he heard a big noise and here comes the dog with a moose hot on his tail. 'Course the dog is coming right to Jim. The moose had one horn knocked off of him already, probably from a fight with another bull. Lucky Jim had his rifle, he nailed him right there.

I had another funny experience with a moose when I was trapping beaver on Hess Creek in late March. We'd just had a big blow and I was headed up the creek to check my sets. The trail was full of snow so my five dogs had a hard time breaking through. I ran behind the sled on snowshoes. They couldn't go very fast anyway so I left my rifle in the sled.

"This is one of my brother's trapping cabins on the West Fork of the Tolovana River in the 40's."

I come around a bend and there was a young cow moose feeding on willows hanging off the bank. Off there browsing. 'Course when she seen the dogs, and the dogs seen her, she run off up the creek. The team made a big lunge and got away from me. I wasn't hanging on the handlebars anyway, but I knew they wouldn't go very far. They were pretty good dogs. They wouldn't leave me.

I come around another long bend where I had a beaver set. Here the dogs were laying right by the beaver house. But before I got there, I hear a noise up on the bank. Big bull up there running back and forth. It was a steep bank, good ten or twelve foot drop, so he couldn't get down on the creek.

He run off in the woods.

By the time I got a couple hundred feet from the sled, this big bull come running out of the brush straight to the sled! 'Course the dogs all whipped around and got tangled up trying to get him. He started running back and forth in the middle of the creek. I headed for the timber, trying to get up the bank and climb a tree or something. The dogs is raising heck and the bull wouldn't leave. He kept running around about fifty feet off from the dogs.

Hair standing up on his shoulders. No horns. They shed their horns in the last part of January. This was March. He was staying on one side pretty much. I had my rifle in the sled. I had to do something. It looked like he was going to get in those dogs and stamp them.

I finally got nerve enough and made a beeline dash for the sled. Got my rifle out and levered a shell in the chamber. I didn't want him. From the fall I had plenty of moose meat so I wouldn't shoot him unless I had to. I touched off a couple rounds close to him and he just shook his head. All at once he whipped around. Took off up the creek like mad. That's the last I seen of him.

Wolves

The only time I ever heard of wolves attacking anybody was when David Tobuk was a little kid. He had a scar on his face from the wounds. All dressed up in caribou clothes the wolf must have thought he was food. It got all excited and one took a bite of his face. That was more or less just an accident. All these horror stories of wolves are pure bull.

Not that there aren't wolves that cause problems. I've had them make off with a whole caribou right out of my cabin. Another time I shot a moose in the fall up Hess Creek and had him hanging by the cabin. I went on the line setting traps up to the main cabin. Coming back I had to run on the creek.

Dogs got excited so I figured there was another moose around. Then we were only twenty-five miles from Livengood, maybe somebody came out to see me. I knew a few guys with dogs. But I didn't see no smoke or nothing.

When I got to the cabin I saw wolf trails everywhere. They had been right up to the meat. Another day and they would have cleaned it up. I guess when they heard me coming they run off. I had a bunch of big traps around there so I stayed around a couple days and set traps in all the trails. But they never did come back all winter.

Talking about wolves, I was out cutting wood by the river. Fred Gustaveson was cutting too and he headed home a bit before I did. Getting a little dusk, I was walking with my .25-20 rifle. I saw Fred just before he made that bend in the road by Hagen's. I started walking faster to catch up and walk into town with him. I got around the bend just about the time a lone wolf stepped out of the brush behind Fred and followed him. That wolf wasn't forty feet behind him. 'Course Fred didn't know it and I couldn't shoot the wolf because he was right in line with him. There's a big meadow there and I thought maybe I could get over to the side and get a shot at the wolf. Then after about three hundred feet the wolf jumped off in the brush before I could get a line on him.

I caught up and said, "Say, Fred, do you know a wolf was around?"

"Yaaaaaaaaa, sure," he said, the old Swede.

Another fella living in Rampart, Clem Anderson, told me one and I know he wasn't lying. It sounds like he was but he wasn't the type of guy to tell a story if it wasn't so. He went up above Rampart to trap before the ice started running in the river. He pitched a tent to live in until he got a cabin built. He finished the cabin in a few weeks. It had one window and a pole bed. Years ago, you know, they used to send bacon in a slab with a tough rind on it. He had one of those bacon rinds hanging from the ridge pole of the tent frame. He was sitting on his bed in the cabin looking out his window and he saw a wolf step out of the brush. That wolf walked right up to the bacon rind. He had smelled that bacon and wanted it. Clem had his rifle standing outside the door. He said he opened the door real easy and reached for the gun. He looked up and the wolf had disappeared back into the brush.

Clem figured the wolf might be back so he set his rifle by his bed. He's sitting in the same place on the bed, looks up, and the wolf is looking through the window at him. He reaches over and takes his rifle real easy. About the time he raises it to sight, the wolf is gone again. He would have shot right though the glass.

Night comes and Clem is sure the wolf is never coming back, but he's still sitting on his bunk. This time with the rifle across his knees. Suddenly he looks up and the wolf is at the window again! He swings the rifle around, but the wolf takes off into the brush. And that's the last time the wolf was around there.

Another story on the wolves. One year I was trapping up Hess and Frank Sisson was trapping below me. He went out early to fix up his trapline. Well, I did that, too. I walked out in October.

I come up to an old cabin some trappers built before the war. It was partly dilapidated, but Frank was staying in it and building a new one next to it. I helped him finish it, of course.

A couple days before I got there, Frank was sitting by a cook fire he had in front of the cabin. There was no stove inside so he cooked over a fire outside. And this wolf comes right up to the fire while he's sitting there. He quick reached over, grabbed his rifle, and nailed the wolf not ten feet away.

"Me and my brother was trapping that winter, maybe '38. That's some wolves and a couple wolverines I caught that year. From the left is Mrs. Maul, she lived up at the sawmill, Harry Havolock from Rampart now, Toots Windish, my brother Frank, me, Lois Isaacson, Mel Maul the guy that had the sawmill at Baker Creek. I got about seven or eight dollars a piece for the wolves and then a twenty dollar bounty for each one."

I come out a couple days later from town and he had just skinned it out, an old black wolf. It had no teeth, so I guess it couldn't rustle for itself. Poor, too, you know. Come right up to that fire. It's hard to figure them out.

Hess Creek

The line I'm talking about up Hess Creek was part of Frank Reinosky's. He made a good living trapping and prospecting up there. Finally he got too old, so he just give up the game. We knew him like you know everybody else. When Jim Pickings and me got out of the army, he told us, "Why don't you go trap up there? That's a good place to trap, little bit of marten and everything.

He had a bunch of cabins but he was gone so long the roofs caved in. We built new ones and chopped out the line where it was grown up with brush. We walked out from Livengood the tenth of August, and by the start of the season we had five new cabins ready to go. All we used to build them was an ax. No window and no door and a double decker pole bed along one wall. Reinosky's cabins were all as big as my house in Manley. The one's Jim and I built were all about ten by ten. We banked them good and used plenty of sod on the roof. They were real warm and comfortable with our tin Yukon stove.

Jim only stayed one year, then his dad asked him to help him with the cattle ranch in Okanogan. He never came back. I kept trapping there for eight years then I walked away and left everything. I just abandoned it, traps and everything. Everything was a tailormade set up. Cabins had stoves and every cabin had saws and axes. I must have left over six hundred traps. That year my brother Frank accidently sliced his leg while gutting a moose and bled to death in his cabin. I had no desire to go back.

My home was always in Manley and nobody was trapping around here so I just moved operations. Horace Roberts trapped across the river. Jimmy Albert was down at the mouth, but I had the rest of this country, up by Baker Creek and in there.

Those days when you had a trapline it was a gentleman's agreement with other trappers. You never went around another guy's line. Especially where guys had established lines with cabins and all. Nobody tried to move in on you. Maybe once in awhile some bird would come in and try to pull something, but not much of that. If someone did, if you was a better man than he was, you moved him out. That was the whole thing. Run him off. Grab him by the collar and shake him up a bit.

Trapping With Dogs

Now it's all different. Sno-gos bring all kinds of trappers. Easy to trap now. Them days you went out and chopped trails, built cabins and everything. Or you took over an empty prospector's cabin. There was a lot of prospecting still going on. No easy money around these places. People would have to go out in the hills and stay there all winter sinking holes. Looking for something. They were all over the country.

Lot of times trappers poled up the river in the fall with their dogs and a tent and didn't come in all winter. When the airplanes got to this country it was a lot easier. I've air dropped my stuff several times. With dogs

Frank Albert preparing food at the N.C. Store for an air drop, circa 1948.

Norm Suckling.

90

it can be a long trip to come into town for groceries sixty miles with a foot of new snow on the trail. Somebody with an airplane can bring your stuff right out.

At that time airplanes didn't cost too much. You could hire a plane for forty bucks an hour that could drop you five hundred pounds of stuff. If the fur wasn't too bad you'd make that up in no time. Otherwise you'd be beating your brains out going into town. All that time in dead work when you could be trapping.

I was trapping up on West Fork one spring and I had to come almost all the way in on bare ground. Hard pulling but we made it. It was breaking up and I had to get in here. The creeks were getting full of water. Not much snow that winter either. Lot of times like that trying to cross creeks in the spring I just have to wait until night, let it cool off so the water will go down. And then sometimes I just have to cache the sled and let the dogs loose. They follow me across however they can.

I was generally traveling pretty light on those trips. I already brought my fur into town and sold it, so I just had my bedding. A lot of times after trapping we'd do a little prospecting. Get on some creek and sink a few holes trying to find something. We'd just stay out. It was fun to live out there, you know, instead of being around town.

I never used a lot of dogs, four or five was my biggest team. But the dogs were all workers, not like these skinny little race dogs now. My dogs were middle-sized at around sixty-five pounds. Some guys, like freighters and mail carriers, had dogs over a hundred pounds for pulling big loads. 'Course trappers were in no hurry. We had to stop

Manley Hot Springs winter dog races 1981. L-r: Michelle McMullen, Eric Meffley, Wess Gurtler, Denise McMullen, unidentified, Pam Redington.

Joee Redington with one of his race dogs at his home in Manley Hot Springs, November 1980.

all the time to check sets, we didn't have to cover that much distance.

Our dog harnesses were different then, too. We had a work collar like an old horse collar with tugs and traces and a singletree behind the dog. He could lean into the collar and really pull. These racing harnesses now are for light work. When a dog really pulls on it it squeezes him, like being in a straitjacket.

This country used to have a lot of cabins scattered around. The government built a lot of them and called them mail cabins, but they were for anybody. Mail drivers used them and so did anybody else traveling the trail. As a rule, guys were pretty good about leaving the cabin cleaned up with a little wood inside and maybe some food. But if you got off the main trail away from the traffic, any cabin you'd come to would have cooking utensils and a good stove, some blankets hanging up and a little grub, coffee, tea, salt, sugar, maybe some rice. If you hit there hungry, there'd be enough to get a few meals. Always matches and wood. Prospectors and trappers most generally never hauled anything out when they left.

When I first came around here the trails were pretty good. You could follow them easy and all the cabins were in good shape. Only in these late years they're all going to hell, roofs caving in and all. People respected the places no matter whose they were. If you took something, you left something. Oh, once in awhile you'd get some bird come through who'd eat up everything, burn all the wood and leave dishes dirty. But everybody knew who he was. You couldn't make a move in this country without people knowing.

When you're trapping with dogs you make a lot of trail sets for wolves and fox because they follow the dogs. So you had no business on somebody else's trail with your team because you just don't know what you'd run into. If a guy cuts his own trail, you got no business on it. I wouldn't set traps on purpose to catch dogs, because I feel sorry for the dog. But another guy has no business on my trails. It's just poor policy to follow somebody else's trail.

But far as roads go, they're public. I wouldn't set traps on it. Take this Tofty Road. Somebody coming over from Tanana with dogs is going to follow the trail and run the road into Manley. I wouldn't set traps there.

Traveling For Fur

If you're in good lynx country and there's lots of rabbits, you can catch plenty of them with snares where they cross creeks and trails. Where I was trapping up Hess it was high country. Not many lynx, it was marten country. Generally you don't find marten where there's lynx. I guess they kill them. Lynx like green timber country. Before the big fire in 1969 there were lynx around here and no marten. Since the brush growed up with berries and mice, the marten moved in. Now there's quite a few caught around here every year.

I came to a lynx crossing once and made three cubbies. All of them were baited with traps and all of them were within sight of each other. Five days later I came back through there and had something in each one. A wolverine was in the first one. He must have gotten caught first or he could have eaten the other two. A lynx was next, and the third had a coyote. Very few coyotes around and as a rule they won't go up to a cubby. Quite a catch.

Not much fur around here now compared to what I've seen. Mostly I guess because there's more trappers. There must be a dozen guys trapping out of here now. You had to go miles and miles to find that many years ago.

It's harder to trap with dogs or by foot like the old timers did. With all the roads and Cat trails around, you can make forty or fifty miles in a day with a snowmachine. Providing it doesn't break down. With dogs you had to build cabins every ten miles or so, or pitch a tent. You have to have long lines and chop out trails.

In the spring I made caches for everything. Rolled up the isinglass window and hung it in a tree. Took the door off and left the place wide open. That way bears just wandered in and wandered back out without tearing the place apart. Lot of times I walked out to my line in middle of September to fix up the cabins and do a little hunting. I had to put things back together, then walk back out to bring a load of grub.

I never had breakdowns when I was driving dogs. They could always get me home. All the cabins had axes and saws. If the team got away from you and crashed into a tree, broke up the sled, you just hewed out another piece and tied it in there. I generally had babiche in my pack for that and fixing snowshoes. No, the only time I walked back was with these iron dogs.

"Jim Rider and Lank Parr in Manley geting ready for trapping. Mike Isaacson was hauling them out to the North Fork of Baker with his pickup." 1938.

I was the second one around here to get a sno-go after Bill Burk. Before that he built himself an air sled. It was driven with an airplane engine and a prop, something like an air boat, but it had skis. He use it quite a bit around the mouth of the Kantishna where he lived, but it was hard on gas. And it couldn't go like a sno-go. You had to stay in open, flat country.

If you've got a good trail and long days in the spring you can make fifty miles a day with dogs. But then you're not trapping, you're traveling. When these guys now tell me they make twenty-five or thirty miles a day all they're doing is traveling. I trapped here since 1934 and you can't tell me that's trapping. When you're in lynx country or fox, you got all kinds of snares set in the trail. You've got to go ahead and set them aside to get through. Then you've got lots of sets off to the side of the trail to check too. If it snows you have to lift the traps up so animals can trigger them. And you got to replace baits the mice get to. It takes a long time to go around the line. Thirty miles a day isn't trapping.

Chapter Five: Army

I knew I was going to be drafted. Everyone else was. Just a matter of time. I put in forty-six months, but all of it was in Alaska. First I was in Ft. Richardson and then around the Aleutians.

You know how the army is. I was always doing something — wrong most of the time. The army was worse on guys like me, older, been on our own, living out in the hills. Young guys twenty or twenty-one don't know any better than to take orders. The war was on. It was for a cause. That's the only reason I went in.

They put all the Alaska guys in the 297th Infantry. They used to call us the "Fighting 297th". We'd go down to the wet PX, get all beered up, and beat up on the 4th Infantry. They say the only battle the 4th Infantry ever lost was to the 297th. Bunch of toughers in there. All trappers, miners, and loggers. Renegades, these common soldiers. They'd go to town and come back when they felt like it, most of them. No passes. I never spent any time in the brig, but I should have been in there lots of times. They just never caught up with me.

They were pretty lenient around Ft. Richardson. Then when we went down to the the islands, there was no place to go. We were stuck on an island. Our outfit was called the Scouts. They'd dump us off on an island and we'd see if there were any Japs on it. Islands were all barren. Not even a bush on most of them. Nothing but grass.

Japs had scouting parties on all those islands too, but their only camps were on Kiska and Attu. I was at Attu when they were fighting down there. Twenty-five of us were in Massacre Bay. We were a reserve. We could see from the bay where they were battling. A bunch from our outfit was in the middle of it.

From there we went to Shemya, another island near Attu. There were supposed to be Japs there, but they already left. I guess they took them off with subs. The Air Corps supposed to have spotted them, but we never found any. We rendezvoused back to our headquarters on Adak and convoyed to Kiska. By the time we got there, the Japs had pulled out.

All the army on those islands was full of Okies, hillbillies from Tennessee and Kentucky. They had a whiskeystill on every island after awhile. There was more moonshine, all those birds from the South, you know. The 807 Engineers had stills going making raisinjack and anything. You could sell anything that had alcohol in it. They pay any price. You could get up to a hundred dollars for a fifth. No other place to spend your money.

Poker was going all the time, too. Finally a half a dozen guys ended up with all the money. Then they'd have these big games. Hell, I seen one guy win $10,000 one night. Me and another guy won $1,000 another night.

That was big money because when I went in I got twenty-one dollars a month. Down in the islands I got thirty dollars. When I got to be a corporal I got seventy dollars a month and that was as high as I went.

I was in the Aleutians twenty-three months. It didn't bother me or the other guys from here. But, gee, those guys from cities like back in New York and all them places. They thought they was at the end of the world in hell. It wasn't tough down there. Oh, it was wet and rainy. You didn't get much to eat. Poor grub and all that. But it didn't bother us guys.

When we first went there, there was nothing in the PX. You couldn't even get tobacco. Later you'd have to stand in line to get a pack of cigarettes or box of snoose. I didn't smoke myself, but I'd get in line for a sack of Bull Durham, snoose, or cigar and give it to my buddies.

Stanley Dayo Collection.

"That's me and George Raufe at Fort Richardson when I was defending the homeland here in the army, 1944.

Nothing but bum grub. No fresh meat around. Just spam and corned beef and hash. I remember one time in Adak we were rationed with the 807 Engineers. A bunch of fresh pork chops came in and those cooks put them all in big kettles and boiled them. I thought there was going to be a riot. I thought we'd have some hanged cooks.

One guy who was a cook, all he knew how to make was hotcakes. He said, "I'm not a cook, I'm a welder. That was my trade." Here they had him in the kitchen.

That's just the way they were. A guy I knew, Harry Larson, was a cook on American Creek here. Born in Alaska and he was a good cook. I mean he could really cook. Like the rest of us he got drafted. After the war, I met him in Fairbanks. He was working for Livengood Placers. I said, "What'd you do in the army?" I thought he'd be in the kitchen cooking.

"I was in the infantry," he said, "I never saw the inside of the kitchen except on KP." And he was a first class cook, that guy.

Another guy, Johnny Evers, was a driller for Cleary Hill. I come in the army and here he's a cook. "Sure, I'm a cook," he said, "this is the best job in the army."

Chapter Six: Nobody's Isolated Anymore

Raising Dixie

There's a lot of people will say, you're out of your mind living out in the woods all winter by yourself trapping. To me it all depends on how you like it. Some want to be around a city. I never was one of them. Then there's all kinds of guys like me want to be out in the woods. They like it out in the woods. People say I must be crazy living out by myself all winter, and stuff. It don't bother me. Even Dixie here. She'd just as soon be out in the woods. It don't bother her.

Always take enough warm clothes. If I got enough warm clothes, I'll never get cold. You can always take it off and put it in the sled if you're moving around too much and start to sweat. Mostly I just use regular wool shirts and pants, canvas parkies, and mooseskin mitts or bearskin mitts, mukluks or good moccasins on my feet. The main thing up in this country to have good hand gear and foot gear. Here in the timber you can always start a fire. 'Course it you get in the arctic where there ain't no timber, you want to make sure you got plenty of fur clothes. If one of them big blows comes and catches Eskimos out on the land, they probably have double caribou skin pants and parkies, so they just crawl in a snow bank and wait it out.

Tanana Valley to the Alaska Range from the top of Bean Ridge overlooking Manley, 1984.

Curt Madison.

Stanley Dayo in his home at Manley Hot Springs November 1981.

Curt Madison.

When I first came around here Natives were making all those fur hats, mitts, parkies, and stuff. Caribou, muskrat, beaver, anything you wanted. I just bought it off of them. The old army had a lot of stuff here, too. Canvas boots with horsehide bottoms were popular. You could get fur liners to put inside. But no matter how warm your boot is, you got to have room to move around. If it's not loose, your feet can freeze easy. If you know how to take care of yourself, the cold won't bother you. 'Course some people can naturally stand more cold.

I started taking Dixie out trapping with me when she was about twelve. She could handle herself pretty good. Better with an ax than some men around here. She didn't go out for any long times in the winter, but summer she spent a lot of time out at the mine.

Liz Woods and Dixie Dayo about age 12. Circa 1968.

Judy Woods and family at Steve Bredeman's potlatch. Judy Woods at far left. Dorothy Shockley, Virginia Woods and Lilly Evans at far right.

Dixie Dayo in front of Stanley's home in Manley Hot Springs 1984.

1956, Stanley holding one month old Dixie in front of logs he got in the spring.

Dixie's birthday at three years old, 1959. Front l-r: Jim Dart, Dixie Dayo, Billy Lanning, Jeannie Blackburn, Mary Lanning. Back: Unidentified, Carol Lee holding baby.

I wanted Dixie to learn how to take care of herself in the woods. I showed her some things and she catches right on. You just have to use good common sense. Like on trapping, Dixie hasn't gone out trapping by herself, but she knows enough that she could do it. Anybody with some common sense can trap. I know a lot of guys raised in big cities turned out to be good trappers. You just got to get out and start doing it. People ask me to explain how to do it, but they just have to go out and look for sign. Can't catch animals if there aren't any around. Anybody can trap marten. There's no skill to that.

It wasn't bad raising Dixie by myself, I got a lot of help from people in town. If I had to go out to work or go trapping, I'd farm her out to different women in town. Betty Fleagle and Judy Woods took a lot of care of her for me. They had kids her age and she was in good care with them. When I'd come in she'd stay with me again. One year I left her with a school teacher and his wife, Jack Murphy. They had four or five kids a little younger than her and they wanted her to look after them a little bit. I never had trouble leaving her with someone if I had to go to work. They knew I had to make a living trapping or whatever. Then she stayed with her brother Darryl up in Fairbanks two or three years going to high school. She didn't care for Fairbanks much so she came back and took correspondence to finish.

Dixie'd go out and cut wood with me. She was never lazy there. In fact she's a lot better than lots of guys around here. She'd pile the wood while I cut or drag it to the truck. Drag the brush out of the way. That's the way she reduces. Chores she'd have to do, she did. No problem. Like when she was younger she got a little hand sled and hauled a couple buckets of water from the hot springs. Never had any trouble getting her to do dishes.

Once she got bigger she watched me cooking and wanted to learn that. I told her what I knew about it. Then she got her own ideas and would read cook books. But then my style is to just throw stuff in till it tastes right. I never follow recipes.

There were lots of kids around when Dixie was growing up. Dart's were a little older, but close. Then Bill Burk had a bunch, and Fleagles and Woods. Lannings had a couple across the slough. Other people moved in once in awhile but they didn't last long. Dixie's got five half-brothers and sisters. I raised them for awhile here.

People Change

I've seen guys working at forty-five below with just canvas gloves. I can stand a lot of cold but that's amazing. And this guy Mel Maul who used to own the mill at Baker went all winter with just one pair of socks and leather shoes. Forty below or not, it didn't bother him.

The hills used to be full of trappers and prospectors. Up and down these rivers and all over, you know. They go out in the fall of the year and never come back until in the spring, till the rivers or creeks break up. That was before the airplane. Now a lot of them fly in or got their own airplanes. Nobody's isolated anymore like they used to be. When you got out 100 miles or 150 miles and you got dogs, you didn't think about coming into town until the season was over and you were done trapping.

People change. Look around here. You don't see hardly anybody going out and staying any more. All these guys that trap got sno-gos. They're gone and home every night. They don't stay out more than one or two nights.

It was different when we trapped. It all depends on how a guy wants to work at it. If that's the way you want to trap, that's the way you do it. If you don't want to stay out, well, come home. When we went out, we stayed.

I used to take a radio out to my home cabin to listen to news and that. Not that it bothered me much to miss it. I was always contented. I didn't miss nothing. I liked what I was doing. I liked to trap and stay out.

Then when me and my brother Frank worked together, he'd go one way and I'd go the other. Every week or five days we'd be together again. Maybe stay a couple days, all depends. A lot of people can't take it. They can't stay by themselves. The percentage is small that can get out and live by themselves. There used to be a lot of those people around Manley. All about the same caliber as we were. We all had the same thing to talk about. I look around now and life is altogether different.

The population is greater in the U.S. and people are spreading out more. But in this vicinity the population is down more than when I first came here. Most of the mining people pulled out for the cities. Easier to make a living. Up and down this river was just full of people, trappers and Natives lived here and there. They're all gone. They all moved to the towns. A lot of people don't want to live out in the hills now. Even the ones that's born here.

Trouble is, now the times are good. You can go into these towns and it's easy to make a living. Big wages and everything. These miners can't pay that kind of wages. The ground ain't that good. And all these give-away programs they got like food stamps. People don't have to work. You can live without working if a guy wants to go that route. When I was growing up you had to get out and make your own living. If you didn't you went hungry. Everybody was working doing something.

Anytime you get something for nothing, it just breaks the people down. Especially the younger ones. When they can get that stuff before they have to go to work, why go to work? That's the attitude they take. There never used to be any relief for guys around here. Sure, when they got old the Territory would pension them off.

There was no hospital care. Native Service hospitals would take Natives and I guess they had to take you if you was desperate. But if you was out on your line and you got sick, it was just too bad if you couldn't make it in. There was a lot of them just swallowed the barrel, committed suicide.

I dragged in one guy here. He had a stroke and he had to do it. It was just tough on them. If they didn't make it in they died out there when they got sick. They've found a lot of guys dead in their cabins. I picked up another guy dead on the West Fork. He got sick and died. Nobody around to take care of him. That happened all the time.

Before they had Social Security, these old loggers moving around and that, when they got old, they had nothing. Only ones with retirement were guys that worked someplace steady day in and day out. Now you can move around and you pay into Social Security with each job.

I never worked a steady job too long. Just enough to get a grubstake — one year or a few months. Then I'd be trapping or prospecting. But every job I paid into Social Security. When you make money mining, your taxes pay into it, too. It's not much to pay and it's one of the best things that ever happened to the working man.

There's lots better conditions now. You've got MediCare. You can go on it now if you're crippled up and not even 65 yet. And they got all these Pioneer Homes. They're good homes. A guy that's been living in the country, something happens to him, they'll take him in there and he'd got real good care. They feed him good. Medical attention and everything.

I can remember years ago, when these old loggers'd get sick, they had nothing. They didn't save no money up, you know. Homes would take them in, but they weren't very good. When the old guys would go in they'd say, "Now they give me the black bottle." You know, get rid of them that way.

You got a lot of benefits now. Veterans from any kind of service are pretty well taken care of. If you get sick, you put in a call and the army comes right out, picks you

Curt Madison.

Stanley in his front yard November 1981.

up and takes you in a chopper. No strings attached.

Gruening got a law passed when he was a senator from Alaska. Since there's no Veteran's Hospitals in Alaska, you can go to any doctor in town and Veteran's will pay for it. I had an operation on my eye under that one. they take good care of you and pretty good pensions if you're really bungged up.

The future don't look too good to me for trapping. There's so much different stuff coming on the market that they don't use fur like they used to years ago. Synthetic stuff, alpaca stuff, feather coats and all that. When I was growing up everything was fur. Now you see a little fur, but nothing like you used to. You can make parkies out of that other stuff, but it's not as good as fur when it comes to the real test. It's not bad, but like in the arctic with all that wind nothing beats fur. You can get by with this other stuff, but it can't take the place of mukluks, polar bear pants, reindeer parkies and that stuff.

Another thing, so many people don't know how to wear fur. If it gets wet they don't know how to dry it out. They'll hang it over the stove and shrivel it all up. This insulated underwear and down and that. It's pretty good, but I spend quite a bit of time myself in the arctic and I know you can't beat fur for being the real thing.

Chapter Seven: Dad

This final chapter is in the words of Dixie, Stanley's daughter.

Wash A Few Boulders

Dad would get that gleam in his eye in the springtime. It was an extra special time of the year because he would get anxious to go gold mining. When the days started getting longer he'd always get real happy to get ready to go. Once he got out to his mine he'd just say he was "going to wash a few boulders." He wouldn't talk about how much gold he was going to get. But, I think once you get gold fever you always have it in your blood that you're going to go out there and do something in the mines.

When he came in from his gold mine, he'd have all these nuggets and money from his big clean-up. Later, if he was working for other people close to Manley, I'd go out with him to the gold mines. Even now he has a mine and goes out there fooling around. I think some of it has washed off in my blood because I look forward to spring and seeing him go out to the mines. I like finding out what's happening out here. Every year he gives me an ounce or two of gold for being his good little girl. So, he's given me quite a bit of gold through the years.

We always worked together because there was only the two of us. He taught me at a very young age how to cook, cut wood and do everything you do in a house. When I was real

Stanley giving Dixie advice on using a gun. April 1984.

Curt Madison.

106

little and went to the mines with Dad I just hung around the cook shack in the morning with the cook. As soon as I was old enough to help, I did the cooking. I always said that I've been cooking since I could reach the knobs on a propane stove. In the afternoons I'd go out on the Cats with Dad and be in the gold mine. I also had to clean out the screens in the pump boxes. I never got tired of being out with him.

Golden Childhood

Dixie's mother Hazel at Lake Minchumina.

My mother was married a couple of times before she was married to my dad so I have three older brothers and two older sisters. They all come down and visit my dad and write him letters. They keep in touch with him. My oldest brother Darryl is a commercial fisherman in Bristol Bay, then there's my brother Robert Thompson everyone calls "Bolo". He lives a subsistence way of life in Lake Minchumina with his wife Jane and their two daughters. My sister Carol Lee is a housewife in Fairbanks. She and her husband have five children. Then there's Jeannie who lives in Wyoming with her husband and three kids. Johnathon who also lives at Lake Minchumina and has a couple sons. They all keep in touch with Dad.

We all lived together as a family for about four years. When I was four my Mom and Dad split up and I started staying with Dad. That was the year before I went to school. When there was just Dad and I, I got all the attention. Whenever we went anywhere I was the only kid because his friends were older and didn't have children so I grew up very spoiled. I think more than the other kids.

"Dixie's brother Bob and I were hauling water, I was practically getting out of the dog business. They were Bob's dogs, 1961.

Dixie's third birthday. L-r: John Dart, Jonathan Blackburn, Jimmy Dart, Holmberg girl, Dixie Dayo, Carol Lee holding baby, Billy Lanning, Jeannie Blackburn, Mary Lanning. 1959.

Dixie, 1960.

I had the golden childhood. Mostly it was Dad. He's a very kind man and friendly with everybody in town. He wasn't moody and everyday was a good one to him. And generous, he'd rather give something away than keep it for himself. I don't think my dad has one enemy to his name. He was always visiting people and taking me with him. So, while he was visiting with his friends they'd be showing me how to do things.

All the women in town were real fond of me when I was a child. I guess they felt sorry for me that I didn't have a mother. They were all nice and friendly and invited me to their houses. One lady taught me how to make blueberry pie and another lady taught me how to make slippers. One taught me how to patch my clothes. Another taught me how to make bread. All these ladies taught me how to make different things. It was just like having a whole bunch of moms. They took the time and just sat me down and showed me how to do things.

Be Honest And Work Hard

He always wanted me to be a good guy. He never wanted me to be one of these people that would take advantage of anyone or cheat them. He always wanted to teach me to give everybody the good end of the deal. Be truthful to people. When you're going to made a deal — make a deal. Be happy with what you come out with. Don't be complaining that the other person got more than you. Just work it out. He always said to be honest and work hard for what you're going to get because no one's going to make it for you except yourself.

He confused me a couple times because he wanted me to know all the ways to do things yet be able to cope in this new world we're in. He wanted me to be more modern than old fashioned. He's into new modern gadgets and is always getting something new. He wanted me to have the best of everything and constantly tried to improve on my lifestyle. He wanted me to be aware that it was a new exciting world and to go out and see what was there. Don't miss out on anything. I don't think he missed out on anything and he didn't want me to.

He never wanted me to be afraid of anything. I don't think I am. Except in the fall, maybe, of the dark. You're not used to the dark and kind of wonder what's out there once the sun quits shining at night. I think Dad made me curious to try different things. He was so full of adventure and always wondering what was around that next creek, up over that other hill or something. He made me adventurous in the same way.

Dad has often said, "I just raised you the best that I knew how, I raised you like a man." He always emphasized that I was to be strong and proud and tough. He wanted me to learn how to take care of myself and know how to get by in this world. He told me that I would take care of him when he was an old man. He emphasized that children should learn how to take care of their parents when they're older so they wouldn't have to go to an old folks home. Of course Dad has never considered himself old. Even though he's seventy-one now, he still acts like a young man.

Curt Madison.

Seventy-one and we still work together the same way we have for years. In the falltime we go out and cut wood and I pack all the wood and he cuts down all the trees. I finally figured it out that cutting is easier than packing. We go out and target practice a lot. We shoot guns. Even though I'm twenty-seven now he insists he shows me one more time so I'll make sure that I do it right.

Dad doesn't like to pick berries too much but he'll

Curt Madison.

Stanley and Dixie 1984.

go out with me so I can pick them. I've been trying to get him to go out moose hunting with me but he says he's slept under enough spruce trees in his time. He doesn't really like to take me hunting too much. I guess he figures that's man's work and women shouldn't be hunters. But he's supposed to go moose hunting with us this fall.

And trapping, he never would show me how to trap. But I've learned these things on my own. My brothers have taught me since Dad wouldn't. We felt it was valuable to know so I just go out with them. Dad's trapped every year that I can remember. He's always had a few snares set out. And always catches a few skins every year. He usually just gives them to me now that he's not doing it for a living, and I'll sew something out of them.

Dad tells me what to do, just like he did when I was a kid. (laugh) I found that it's so much easier to just listen to what he has to say because he knows all kinds of neat things and if you do them the way he says they usually work out a lot better. I started really paying attention and we get along real well if I do things the way he says. Like putting wood in my stove. Everyday when he comes to my house he checks my fire. If I don't have the wood in my stove the right way, he rearranges it and explains the way the fire should be burning. So he just keeps telling me things until I do them the way he wants them done.

Even though he says I'm going to take care of him when he's old, he still takes care of me like I was a child. I let him do it because he enjoys it. But I have to be real careful that he doesn't come over here and start doing everything in my house. He's ambitious, and will even do my dishes for me. It kind of makes me feel bad when he does my dishes because I figure I'm old enough to be doing them. He just wants to help out as much as he can. He always wants to be doing something. When he sits around too much he gets real nervous. He wants to keep moving.

It's hard to talk about Dad. He was a great father — is a great father. He's been helpful, encouraging and a real proud man. He sure loves me, I know that.

Manley Hot Springs 1983. The large clearing is the airport and old Sabin ranch.

Manley residents watch the Tanana River from the Landing as it begins to flood the bank, spring 1982.

The Manley Roadhouse 1984.

The Ramona Barge at the Manley Hot Springs Landing 1984. L-r on the Ramona: Claude Demientieff Sr. on top, Rudy Demientieff, Sean Carney, Claude Jr.

Yvonne Yarber and Stanley Dayo looking at photos for this book in Stanley's home, November 1981.

Index

Curt Madison.

Stanley Dayo in his home at Manley Hot Springs November 1981.

The *Yukon-Koyukuk Biography* Series

Available from Spirit Mountain Press

Edgar Kallands - Kaltag	**$6.95**
Josephine Roberts - Tanana	**$6.95**
Billy McCarty - Ruby	**$6.95**
Simeon Mountain - Nulato	**$8.95**
Altona Brown - Ruby	**$14.95**
The Darts - Manley Hot Springs	**$9.95**
Goodwin Semaken - Kaltag	**$9.95**
Henry Ekada - Nulato	**$7.95**

Coming Soon:

Peter John - Minto
Al Wright - Minto
Martha Joe - Nulato

POSTAGE AND HANDLING

Add $1.00 for first book, 50ᶜ for each additional book. Orders of 10 or more, shipping will be billed.

Send order to:

Spirit Mountain Press
P.O. Box 1214   Fairbanks, Alaska 99707

Stanley Dayo's Family Tree

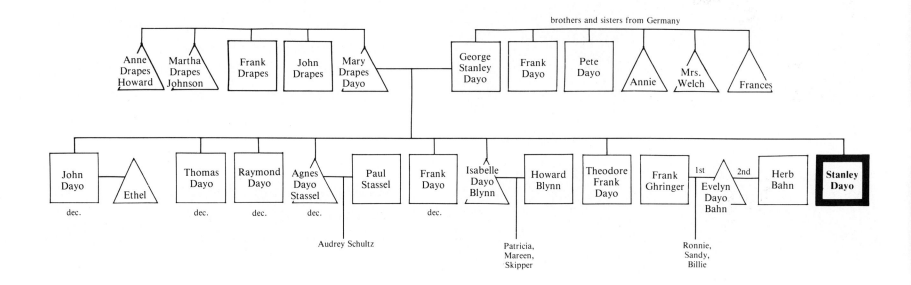

brothers and sisters from Germany

Anne Drapes Howard | Martha Drapes Johnson | Frank Drapes | John Drapes | Mary Drapes Dayo | George Stanley Dayo | Frank Dayo | Pete Dayo | Annie | Mrs. Welch | Frances

John Dayo — Ethel | Thomas Dayo | Raymond Dayo | Agnes Dayo Stassel | Paul Stassel | Frank Dayo | Isabelle Dayo Blynn | Howard Blynn | Theodore Frank Dayo | Frank Ghringer — 1st — Evelyn Dayo Bahn — 2nd — Herb Bahn | **Stanley Dayo**

dec.   dec.   dec.   dec.   dec.

Audrey Schultz

Patricia, Mareen, Skipper

Ronnie, Sandy, Billie

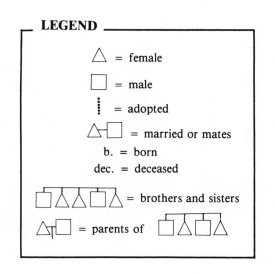

LEGEND

△ = female

□ = male

⋮ = adopted

△—□ = married or mates

b. = born

dec. = deceased

□△△□△ = brothers and sisters

△┬□ = parents of □△△

116